A thought for every day

A thought for everyday from Henry Drummond

Fleming H. Revell Company
Old Tappan, New Jersey

First published by the Drummond Press
Drummond House, 64 Murray Place
Stirling, Scotland
© The Trustees of the Stirling Tract Enterprise

Library of Congress Cataloging in Publication Data

Drummond, Henry, 1851–1897.
A thought for every day from Henry Drummond.

First published in 1972 under title: A mirror
set at the right angle.
Includes bibliographical references.
1. Devotional calendars.   I. Title.
[BV4811.D7   1973]   242'.2   72–10938
ISBN 0–8007–0575–0

FOR

PHILIP SYDNEY HENMAN

A Steadfast Encourager in the Lord

Preface

The work of Henry Drummond—evangelist, author, lecturer—has been read by many over the years. This compilation, organized by John Birkbeck as daily readings, will bring pleasure not only to many who have known and enjoyed his words in the past, but to many first-time readers as well.

Henry Drummond's writings are not new to our company. His devotional book, THE GREATEST THING IN THE WORLD, was first handled by the Fleming H. Revell Company in 1956. Over 235,000 copies have been sold in hardcover and paper in the seventeen years since. It is a love story—the story of love as revealed in the thirteenth chapter of First Corinthians—a simple, stirring love story which was always at the heart of Henry Drummond's message to his many listeners and readers.

The material in this book is organized so that it may be used for daily reading or for topical reference. We are sure you will find that the words of Henry Drummond will live in your hearts and minds as a source of inspiration and hope.

THE PUBLISHERS

Introduction

IT does not belittle the reputation of great saints like Augustine, Bernard, and Francis to maintain that for honest thinking and joyful practice of religion, Henry Drummond merits equal veneration.

The volcanic rock on which the history-saturated castle is perched and the town of Stirling fastens itself, slopes down to the field of Bannockburn where Scotland's champion, Robert the Bruce, won a distinctive place in the nation's story. Nestling amid the crags of that gradient, beneath a tall granite Celtic Cross, rests the mortality of one reckoned the patron saint of youth in the latter part of the 19th century and who was affectionately dubbed "St. Henry of Stirling" by the many in whose interest he spent his life. On the great day of reckoning it will be found that the countless thousands led to God through his spoken word, his written word, and the eloquence of his character, will far outnumber the achievement of even the national hero, the Bruce.

In Drummond's own day it was widely recognised that thousands of young men and women and children—ministers, doctors, teachers, lawyers, merchants, of all professions and occupations, scholars and students, scattered all over the world, owed the growing spiritual stimulus of their lives—under God—to this "the most perfect Christian I have ever seen or expect to see this side of the grave," as confessed one who knew him many years. He died young in 1897.

There now exists a generation almost wholly unaware of this man who was God's lasting benediction to the entire community. Occasionally, it is true, he is quoted today in sermons and theological discourses, yet the impoverishing fact remains that he is scarcely known. Who was he? What did he do? Why ought he to be read by everyone? What was there about him that made a woman come to him on a Saturday evening pleading, "My husband is deein', sir; he's no able to speak to you, and he's no able to hear you, but I would like him to hae a breath o' you afore he dies"?

If one may blurb in the manner of book reviews, read what his contemporaries say of the man, his message, his writings, his influence. "No man had a profounder interest in human nature" . . . "His presentation of truth receives a hearty welcome" . . . "At the heart of all lay his profound reverence, his unreserved acceptance of Christ and of Christ's idea and law of life" . . . "There is no man of our time, be he statesman, philosopher, poet, or novelist, whose words have been more widely read, or read with intenser eagerness, and greater spiritual profit. So singular a combination of gifts as he possessed will not be found twice in a century" . . . "It could be said of him truthfully, as was said of the early apostle, 'that men took knowledge of him, that he had been with Jesus'." A tough journalist, cynically bent, listened in a small mission hall where Drummond was speaking. "I forget the message, but I have since heard it often, and I have never listened to him without recalling the lines:

"I have heard many speak but this one man—
So anxious not to go to heaven alone—
This one man I remember."

Henry Drummond was born in Stirling on August 17, 1851. His immediate forebears were recognised locally for two reasons—they were sons of the soil, Seedsmen by profession, and they showed a zeal for things spiritual yet retaining an independence touching matters of religion and the Church. Grandfather William Drummond not only strove to have his 13 children brought up in the "fear and admonition of the Lord" but also concerned himself with the moral and spiritual needs of neighbours. This latter interest caused him to be haled before the Stirling magistrates charged with setting up a Sunday School in a nearby village and so interfering with the prerogative of the Church. Uncle Peter Drummond diverted his religious interest into a different channel. Distressed by the desecration of the Sabbath and finding his verbal appeals of little avail, he printed a tract which produced the desired effect and which established an evangelical publishing concern which has continued for 125 years. Henry's father, after whom he was named, only blossomed into mature Christian work when he was fifty. He taught in a Sunday School, led every philanthropic cause in the area, was director of the Y.M.C.A., Church Elder, and Justice of the Peace. His appearance and bearing, his silver-toned voice and his "pawky" humour were noteworthy. His mother, Jane Blackwood of Kilmarnock, by her prayers and sweet influence, ensured that the son of the seedsman would be carefully tended in a nursery of piety. His mother's brother, James Blackwood, a great favourite of the boy Henry, was a minerologist and scientific inventor of repute. Such then was the rock from which Henry Drummond was hewn and from such was shaped one born to make men think and see a Christianity which was perfectly normal.

The growing child was characterised by a lively nature, a brisk mind, and a sunny disposition. His first religious challenge came at the tender age of nine. He attended a meeting for children in Uncle Peter's drawing-room and when the others left at the end he stayed behind to speak to his uncle. What all was exchanged we have no record but one snippet exists: "He was weeping to think that he had never loved the dear Saviour who took the punishment he deserved. We prayed together, and he gave his heart to Jesus." Years later, when replying to the award of a Doctorate of Laws at Amherst College, Henry Drummond confirmed that it was at this meeting in his uncle's home that he began to love the Saviour and became a happy Christian.

His enthusiasm for life and his abounding energy found outlet in many adventurous and healthy ways. A keen sportsman, he would be on the cricket field, the football pitch, fishing, rowing, skating, mountaineering, with or without inducement. His heart was filled with laughter and his mind searching after what was genuine. An avid reader, he read deeply and widely those authors who had experimented in and experienced the art of living. The first book he ever bought out of his carefully hoarded savings was a selection from John Ruskin's writings. *"This man taught me to see,"* was a testimony Drummond made often in his addresses to students. The little boy who had been puzzled by the ugliness of nature, the dinginess of the world about, began to learn from Ruskin that Nature blended all that belonged to her with the most perfectly beautiful colouring—"God's first mercy to the world."

On the eve of his fifteenth birthday he left school fired by love for geology and science. Within was conflict for he had felt long that he was "called" of God for service. Curiously, there was no impelling summons to the ministry, and it was only at the insistence of his father that he went to Edinburgh to graduate (contemporary with Robert Louis Stevenson) in Arts. He was not the conventional student and, whether in jest or sympathetic encouragement, once told students in Melbourne, Australia, that he was a "duffer" at college. There are some of his year who recall his leaving College in a cab filled with prizes for science. Others of his student days remember his standing in the quadrangle, apart from the knot of pupils, looking like "one possessed by great thoughts which were polarising in his mind and giving happy expression to his face."

In the autumn of 1873 he returned from a semester at Tubingen, Germany, resolved to leave New College, Edinburgh, and its theological studies for a year and to devote himself entirely to natural sciences and to gain experience in mission work. It is told that on a chilly March midnight two students paced the esplanade of Edinburgh Castle and became engrossed in debate as to the relation between the natural and that indefinable spiritual which seemed to envelop each other. Could it be that the spiritual and natural were but one and the same thing seen from different standpoints? "May not one *law* run through the natural and spiritual?" Drummond asked his companion. A glimpse of the vision which challenged his thinking and ripened into a conception with which his name is unforgettably associated had been caught.

At the comparatively young age of 26 he was appointed a science lecturer in Glasgow where, it is said, he combined three incompatible things—prayer, science, and mesmerism. His versatility often found him rounding off a serious lecture with an acquired exhibition of mesmerism at the expense of some unfortunate victim. Legend has it that one was so under his influence that whenever he met Drummond in the street he would offer him his watch.

In days when the four quarters of the world were far straddled and transport incommodious and slow, Drummond was an inveterate traveller. The first of three visits to the

United States of America took place in 1879 when he accompanied the very distinguished geologist, Professor Sir Archibald Geikie, on a survey of the Rocky Mountains. "He looked on everything with the eye of a poet first, and a man of science afterwards," affirmed Geikie. Little wonder that Drummond's books arising out of his journeyings are rich in descriptiveness. The fruits of a discerning eye are found amply in colourful language.

Journeying to Central Africa to make a survey for a Trading Company, he found many conscious awakenings in his spiritual growth and understanding. "I cherish no more sacred memory of my life than that of a communion service in the Bandawé chapel, when the sacramental cup was handed to me by the bare black arm of a native communicant." While he was in Africa, one thousand miles away from the nearest post office, word eventually came to the effect that he was the most talked-of-man in the religious world of that day. His first literary effort, *Natural Law in the Spiritual World*, had been published in London. This book created a sensation among critics who welcomed the freshness of the style and the relevance of the material. Every minister who wanted to be "with it" preached on the theme-text of the book, "He that hath the Son hath life: he that hath not the Son hath not life," and punctuated it with scientific terms such as "biogenesis," "classification," "organic and inorganic," "degeneration," "semi-parasitism," and "parasitism." Evangelists developed into exponents of conversion, sanctification, and other doctrinal terms using scientific labels. At one revival service a Latin tag of Drummond's was used—*omne vivum ex vivo* (all life comes from life).

Other tours to Australia, the New Hebrides, Java, Malaysia, Japan, and many places in Europe were undertaken by invitation and in the interest of young men.

The God of All Surprises intervened dramatically and directed the talents of Drummond to complement those of Dwight L. Moody and Ira D. Sankey who arrived in Liverpool in 1872 to find that the sponsor for an evangelistic tour of Britain had died. Drummond, who had long advocated and pioneered personal evangelism, was more than normally interested. He went to hear them both and knew that he had to be identified with them. After some reluctance to join them permanently as Moody wished, he unhesitatingly gave them twenty months campaigning from Kirkwall to London. Drummond's own genius for speaking to and captivating young folk and students found him mainly occupied with such audiences. The shoe-salesman from Chicago and the scientist initiated a love and understanding for each other which gallantly stood the criticism and hostility which came from quarters most unexpected. David and Jonathan could not have been more mutually appreciative of each other. Drummond deemed Moody "the biggest human I have ever met" . . . "who only knew two books, the Bible and Human Nature. Out of these he spoke; and because both are books of life, his words were afire with life; and the people to whom he spoke, being real people, listened and understood." Later, when many evangelicals looked with disdain on Drummond's writings, and especially *The Ascent of Man*, asserting that it was "The Descent of Drummond," it was Moody who sprang to the unnecessary defence of Drummond. In reply to the attacks on the supposed heterodoxy, Moody vindicated: "I have read every line of his books, and have never read a word with which I disagreed." Let us not forget Sankey in all this. When the controversy was at its bitterest, he wrote Drummond in Glasgow and enclosed a newspaper cutting of an address given by the Scot. It was a statement of belief about which Sankey sought re-affirmation. It read:

"The power to set the heart right, to renew the springs of affection, comes from Christ. The sense of the infinite worth of the single soul, and the recoverableness of man at his worst, are the gifts of Christ. The freedom from guilt, the forgiveness of sins, come from Christ's Cross; the hope of immortality springs from Christ's grave . . . Personal conversion means for life a personal religion, a personal trust in God, a personal debt to Christ, a personal dedication to His cause. These, brought about how you will, are supreme things to aim at, supreme losses if they are missed."

Drummond's reply from his home, 3 Park Circus, Glasgow, and dated April 3, 1892, reads—"These *are* my words, and there has never been an hour when the thoughts which they represent were not among my deepest convictions. Nor, as far as I know, have I ever given anyone ground to believe otherwise, nor is there any one of my writings which these same ideas will not be found either expressed or understood. My message lies among the forgotten truth, the false emphasis, and the wrong accent. To every man his work "

One must resist the temptation to recount more from the association of Moody and Drummond for the stories are legion. Yet one fragrant episode must be shared. A large gathering of specially invited people assembled on a lawn in Kent to hear Moody. The American began with a very human plea to the effect that after eight months solid preaching he felt "he gave all I have to give" and that he had a substitute just returned from Africa, Henry Drummond. Withdrawing his pocket Bible, Drummond quietly read 1st Corinthians 13, and went on confidently and cogently to make this great Hymn of Love live with vibrant thought and challenge. So was given for the first time this treasure in the devotional literature of mankind—*The Greatest Thing in the World*. Moody was later moved to say this: "Some men take an occasional journey into the thirteenth of 1st Corinthians, but Henry Drummond was a man who lived there constantly, appropriating its blessings and exemplifying its teachings. As you read what he terms the analysis of love, you find that all its ingredients were interwoven into his daily life, making him one of the most lovable men I have ever known."

It is incontestable that in an age which wanted to see *religion lived out*, they saw it in the transparent character of this radiant Christian reflecting the sunshine of the faith. Those who write about him are at one in the conviction that the greatest thing about the man was the man himself. Men felt instinctively that what he said was true to the man who uttered it and that he was telling them of things through which he had lived and which were real to themselves.

There is an undoubted resurgence of interest in the writings of Henry Drummond. Post-graduate research by students in quest of a Doctorate of Philosophy thesis centre on two aspects of the many varied gifts of Drummond—his power of communication and his scientific approach to theology. In a world of unrest and protest against many of the established traditions and accepted beliefs, many are learning that Drummond is articulating clearly what many young people are feeling and saying or wanting to say. It is no accident that the writings of the French geologist-priest, Pierre Teilhard de Chardin, are enjoying such a vogue and causing intelligent minds to ponder the evolutionary development of the human being. Traversing millions of years, de Chardin paints the picture of a grand design from molecules to men and from men to God, the centre of centre; and he expresses his mystical faith: that somewhere around us, in one form or another, some excess of personal, extra-human energy should be perceptible to us if we look carefully, and should reveal to us the great Presence.

But Drummond said this eighty years ago and in simpler, less abstruse wording. Theologically, his great contribution was to build a new and firm bridge across the gulf between scientific and spiritual experience. He believed that "theology proceeds by asking science what it demands, and then borrows its instruments to carry out the improvements." His presentation of theology made it appear a new discovery; it satisfied the doubter and gave hope to the man who was down. After his Lowell Lecture on "The Ascent of Man," considerable discussion arose in the General Assembly of the Free Church. Fortunately, it was saved from branding as a heretic one of the most pious and Christlike men in the Kingdom of God. As an observer put it: "You might as well have beaten a spirit with a stick as prosecute Drummond for heresy."

Those were days—not unlike our own—when many said with Schiller: "In order to reconcile science and religion finally you must be prepared to say what is science and what is religion."

Drummond was not blind to this: he was too much of a realist to ignore the obvious. He did not begin with doctrine and work downwards to nature but ran up natural law as far as it could reach, and then the doctrine burst into view. You don't start with a creed; you arrived at a creed. Evolution was "God's way of doing things." It is the continuous progressive change—"First the blade, then the ear, after that the full corn in the ear" (*The Ascent of Man*). Up to this time no word had come from any source to reconcile Christianity with Evolution, or Evolution with Christianity. And why not, since the two are one. What is Evolution? A method of creation. What is its object? To make perfect living beings. Through what does Evolution work? Through love. Through what does Christianity work? Through love. Evolution and Christianity have the same author, the same end, the same spirit. There is no rivalry between these processes. This, in miniature, is a digest of *The Ascent of Man*. If Evolution reveals anything, if Science itself proves anything, it is that Man is a spiritual being, and that the direction of his long career is towards an even larger, richer, and more exalted life. His two scientific works, *Natural Law in the Scientific World* and *The Ascent of Man*, are an application of many of the current scientific ideas of his day to religious belief and experience. Both books are worthy of the closest intellectual scrutiny today, for although some of his knowledge has been superseded by great strides in technical and scientific know-how, the basic apprehensions of Drummond remain satisfying to reason, amenable to understanding. Drummond would hasten his "Amen" to Wernher von Braun, the Space Scientist, when he said: "It is as difficult to understand a scientist who does not acknowledge the presence of a superior rationality behind existence of the universe as it is to comprehend a theologian who would deny the advance of science." In a day when science of the real sort is slowly learning to walk humbly with God, when there is no conflict between science and religion but only between science and dogmatic theology, when people say that God is dead but it is not the scientists who are saying it, when the best scientists recognise that they are but kindergarten folk playing with mysteries as their ancestors were and their descendants will be, it is a wonderful and encouraging thing to read and re-read Drummond who was a Christian by the laboratory method of experience. He saw that science without religion was blind and did not know where to go, and that religion without science was lame, it did not know how to go: he sought to make plain the dependence of each on the other.

His literary work is marked by a natural felicity and grace of style, simple, sweet, and clear, which won the attention of learned and unlearned alike. Marvellously arresting, epigrammatic, not a dull line anywhere, saturated with a magnetic influence which quickens the pulse, stirs the heart, makes for restlessness to produce the spirit and tone and temper of the writing in your own life. It has been claimed that no books in the language are more calculated to fill one with an over-mastering passion to be something, and to do something for Christ.

"The business of the preacher," said Drummond, "is not to prove things but to make people see them." Even in cold print after all these years, it is apparent that Drummond's preaching was no spiritual aspirin giving temporary relief but a getting down to the real trouble and headache. The simplicity and frankness of his message, the fact that he narrowed down the issue to an unreserved acceptance of Christ as Saviour, his insistence on a true conversion that meant turning from sinful ways and committing themselves absolutely to Christ— Drummond did not mince words when he spoke of the sins of men—gave them assurance that he was dealing with the realities and not the superficialities of human experience, and went home to the conscience and to the heart. They saw before their eyes the embodiment of the life and character and usefulness which the speaker was recommending, and when they conversed with him afterwards they found not only a heart overflowing with sympathy for their temptations and aspirations, but a mind able to evaluate the situation and afford the most shrewd and practical counsel. His chief aim here, as in every other department of his ministry as university professor and as Christian evangelist, was to make men and women think. He rarely touched the emotions. To make them think, to influence the judgment and the will, to persuade the soul, to help them to realise that the service of God was a reasonable service—that was the passion of his sole ambition. He believed in instant delivery from sin and that no man need stay as he is. Failure was not final while the known grace of God was present to be taken and used. He appealed to the heroic element in a man's character, and warned him, in view of the possibility of rising to a higher life, against remaining an example of arrested growth of spiritual development. While so many other preachers feared lest men should lose their souls, Drummond was anxious that they should not miss their lives. The programme of Christianity was for Drummond a great Surrender, a great Obedience, and a great Intimacy. The heart of his teaching is summed up in this beautiful story he told.

"There lived once a young girl whose perfect grace of character was the wonder of those who knew her. She wore on her neck a gold locket which no one was ever allowed to open. One day, in a moment of unusual confidence, one of her companions was allowed to touch its spring and learn its secret. She saw these words: 'Whom having not seen I love.' That was the secret of her beautiful life. She had been changed into the same image."

Henry Drummond had seen his need of a Saviour and saw that Saviour in Jesus Christ. He loved and the image of the eternal Love was reflected in him and through him to thousands in many lands.

At the meridian of 46 he went to behold the face of Him whom he loved and reflected. A malignant disease of the bones affected his spine and for two years he was bound to intense suffering. He could scarce endure the touch of a friendly hand. On March 7, 1897, his friend and physician, Dr. Hugh Barbour, played several hymn tunes to Drummond. There was no obvious response. Then he struck an old favourite, "Martyrdom," and sang the words of Paraphrase 54—"I'm not ashamed to own my Lord." Drummond kept time on the couch with his hand. When the third verse was reached, he joined the others, singing confidently:

"I know that safe with Him remains,
protected by His pow'r,
What I've committed to His trust,
till the decisive hour."

"Nothing can beat that, Hugh," he said at the close. After prayer for their friends, Drummond concluded, "It will all come out right, Hugh."

His spirit returned to God who gave it in His providence for his generation and for the unending ages wherever men and women can read, think, know themselves, and choose the more excellent way of Love—from God, through God to others.

On a day rampant with rain and sleet, they buried him beside his father. Leading men of religion and science, ordinary folk from all walks of life, congregated to thank God for this man who made God bigger and clearer for them and whose gifts and life were a mirror set at the right angle imaging Christ.

—JOHN BIRKBECK.

This book has been compiled because there is a need for the timeless truth extracted from Henry Drummond's literary works, letters, and addresses. It has the distinct potential of achieving two things:

1 To cause the mind so see, the heart to rejoice, and the life to be committed to Christ.

2 To encourage the reader of these devotional extracts to go direct to the complete writings of Henry Drummond and find there what the compiler found in his studying of the style and content—a challenge, a reinforcement, a cleansing.

The devotional extracts are set forth to cover the Christian Year although not tabulated for the ready reason that, as yet, the dates are moveable.

The bracketed number at the end of each quotation refers to the source and this number corresponds with the list of sources found at the end of the book.

January 1   **Attitude of Faith**

The eternal life, the life of faith, is simply the life of the higher vision. Faith is an attitude—a mirror set at the right angle. (1)

January 2   **God-consciousness**

Do we carry about with us a sense of God? Do we carry the thought of Him with us wherever we go? If not, we have missed the greatest part of life. Do we have that feeling and conviction of God's abiding presence wherever we go? (8)

January 3   **Facing the Future**

And when the time of trial comes, and all in earth and heaven is dark and even God's love seems dim: what is there ever left to cling to but this will of the willing heart, a God-given, God-ward bending will, which says amidst the most solemn and perplexing viscissitudes of life:

> "Father, I know that all my life
> Is portioned out for me;
> The changes that are sure to come
> I do not fear to see;
> I ask Thee for a present mind,
> Intent on pleasing Thee." (6)

January 4   **Life's Object**

If we realise that we come into the world to do the will of God and set the helm steady from the beginning, our lives would work out to a great purpose. The real object of life is simply to do the will of God. (7)

January 5   **Life Abundant**

Christianity offers a young man, or an old man, or any man, a more abundant life than the life he is living—more life as life goes; more happiness in life, more intensity in life, more worthiness in life. (16)

January 6   Character-building

We cannot dream perfect character; we do not get it in our sleep; it comes to us as muscle comes, through doing things. Character is the muscle of the soul, and it is developed by the practice of the muscles, and by exercising it upon actual things; hence our work is the making of us, and it is by and through our work that the great Christian graces are communicated to our soul. (8)

January 7   God Speaks . . . Today

When God speaks He speaks so loud that all the voices of the world seem dumb. And yet when God speaks He speaks so softly that no one hears the whisper but yourself. Today, perhaps . . . (6)

January 8   The Supreme Good

What is the *summum bonum*—the supreme good? You have life before you . . . "Love is the fulfilling of the law." It is the rule for fulfilling all rules, the new commandment for keeping all the old commandments, Christ's one secret of the Christian life. (21)

January 9   Reflective Love

Contemplate the love of Christ, and you will love. Stand before that mirror, reflect Christ's character, and you will be changed into the same image from tenderness to tenderness. There is no other way. You cannot love to order. You can only look at the lovely object, and fall in love with it, and grow into likeness to it. And to look at this Perfect Character, this Perfect Life. Look at the great sacrifice as He laid down Himself, all through life, and upon the Cross of Calvary; and you must love Him. And loving Him, you must become like Him. Love begets love. (21)

January 10   **The Lightened Burden**

Christ saw that men took life painfully. To some it was a weariness, to others a failure, to many a tragedy, to all a burden and a pain. How to carry this burden of life had been the whole world's problem. It is still the whole world's problem. And here is Christ's solution: "Carry it as I do. Take life as I take it. Look at it from My point of view. Interpret it upon My principles. Take My yoke and learn of Me, and you will find it easy. For My yoke is easy, sits right on the shoulders, and *therefore* My burden is light." (23)

January 11   **The Ideal Man**

Some years ago, when I was a student, I started out to find the meaning of life, to discover what was the ideal life, and I went for my information to this Book, where I found a sketch of an ideal man . . . "A man after My own heart who shall fulfil all My will." (7)

January 12   **Life-changing**

Not more certain it is that it is something outside the thermometer that produces a change in the thermometer, than it is something outside the soul of man that produces a moral change upon him. That he must be susceptible to that change, that he must be a party to it, goes without saying; but that neither his aptitude nor his will can produce it, is equally certain . . . Growth is not voluntary, it takes place, it happens, it is wrought upon matter, so here, "Ye must be born again"— we cannot *born* ourselves. "Be not conformed to this world, but *be ye transformed.*" We are subjects to a transforming influence, we do not transform ourselves. (1)

January 13   **Road to Life**

If a man could make himself humble to order, it might simplify matters; but we do not find that this happens. Hence death, death to the lower self, is the nearest gate and the quickest road to life. (23)

January 14   Who are Christ's?

Thank God the Christianity of today is coming nearer the world's need! Live to help that on. Thank God men know better by a hair's-breadth what religion is, what God is, who Christ is, where Christ is! Who is Christ? He who fed the hungry, clothed the naked, visited the sick. And where is Christ? Where?—whoso shall receive a little child in My name, receiveth Me. And who are Christ's? Every one that loveth is born of God.   (21)

January 15   School of Christ

I do not say, remember, that the Christian life to every man, or to any man, can be a bed of roses. No educational process can be this. And perhaps if some men knew how much was involved in the simple "learn" of Christ, they would not enter His school with so irresponsible a heart. For there is not only much to learn, but much to unlearn.   (23)

January 16   Condition of Entrance

The first step in religion is for man to feel his helplessness. Christ's first beatitude is to the poor in spirit. The condition of entrance into the spiritual kingdom is to possess the child-spirit—that state of mind combining at once the profound helplessness with the most artless feeling of dependence.   (22)

January 17   Cut and Dry Truth

You cannot cut and dry truth. You cannot accept truth ready-made without it ceasing to nourish the soul as truth. You cannot live on theological forms without becoming a parasite and ceasing to be a man.   (22)

January 18   Narrowness Rebuked

There is nothing the least narrow about anything that Christ ever said. On the contrary, Christ said the broadest things that have ever been said; and He never rebuked breadth, but constantly rebuked narrowness.   (16)

January 19   Seek it First!

And if you gentlemen are going to seek the Kingdom of God, I want to ask you to seek it first. Do not touch it unless you promise to seek it first. I promise you a miserable life and influence and a poor, broken, lost career, if you seek it second. Seek it first, or let it alone. Do not be an amphibian. No man can serve two masters, and if you only knew it, it is a thousand times easier to seek first the Kingdom of God than to seek it second.   (16)

January 20   Science and God

Science has nothing finer to offer Christianity than the exaltation of its supreme conception—God. Science has not found a substitute for God.   (20)

January 21   Flat and Unprofitable?

I meet another set of men who tell me that they don't like churches, that they find sermons stale, flat and unprofitable. Now, if any man here hates a dull sermon, I am with him . . . I think the world is far too dull, and that is one of the greatest reasons why the brightest men should throw themselves into Christianity to give it a broader phase to other people.   (11)

January 22   Life's One Charge

The Image of Christ that is forming within us—that is life's one charge. Let every project stand aside for that. "Till Christ be formed" no man's work is finished, no religion crowned, no life has fulfilled its end. Is the infinite task begun? When, how, are we to be different? Time cannot change men? Christ can. Wherefore, *put on Christ*.   (1)

January 23   Being Carnally Minded

To be carnally minded is death. We do not picture the possessor of this carnal mind as in any sense a monster. We have said he may be high-toned, virtuous, and pure. The plant is not a monster because it is dead to the voice of the bird; nor is he a monster who is dead to the voice of God. The contention at present simply is that he is *dead*.   (22)

January 24   Life . . . Definite
Life is not one of the homeless forces which promiscuously inhabit space, or which can be gathered like electricity from the clouds and dissipated back again into space. Life is definite and resident; and spiritual life is not a visit from a force, but a resident tenant in the soul. (22)

January 25   Rest is Causal
It is no use proposing finely devised schemes, or going through general pious exercises, in the hope that somehow rest will come. The Christian life is not casual but causal. All nature is a standing protest against the absurdity of expecting to secure spiritual effects, or any effects, without the employment of appropriate causes. (23)

January 26   Look! . . . There!
Sunlight is stored in every leaf, from leaf through coal, and it comforts us thence when days are dark and we cannot see the sun. Christ shines through men, through books, through history, through nature, music, art. Look for Him there. (1)

January 27   True Religion
True religion is no milk-and-water experience. It is a fire. It is a sword. It is a burning, consuming heat, which must radiate upon everything around. The change to the Christlike life, is so remarkable that when one really undergoes it, he cannot find words in common use by which he can describe the revolutionary character. He has to recall the very striking phrases of the New Testament, which once seemed such exaggerations: "A new *man*, a new *creature*, a new *heart*, a new *birth*." (6)

January 28   Tempted to Question
The world is a sphinx. It is a vast riddle—an unfathomable mystery; and on every side there is temptation to questioning. God has planned the world to incite men to intellectual activity. (28)

January 29   **Faith v Reason?**

Faith is never opposed to reason in the New Testament; it
is opposed to sight.   You will find that a principle worth
thinking over.   *Faith is never opposed to reason in the New
Testament, but to sight.*   (28)

January 30   **History's Touching Sight**

Surely it is the most touching sight of the world's past to
see God's only-begotten Son coming down . . . to teach the
stammering dumb inhabitants of this poor planet to say, "Our
Father."   (27)

January 31   **Only Worth-while Thing**

To become like Christ is the only thing in the world worth
caring for, the thing before which every ambition of man is
folly, and all lower achievement vain.   (1)

February 1   **Law of Influence**

It was reserved for Paul to make the supreme application
of the Law of Influence.   It was a tremendous inference to make,
but he never hesitated.   He himself was a changed man; he
knew exactly what had done it; it was Christ . . .   On the
Damascus road they had met, and from that hour his life was
absorbed, in His.   The effect could not but follow—on words,
on deeds, on career, on creed.   The "impressed forces" did
their vital work.   He became like Him Whom he habitually
loved.   "So we all," he writes, "reflecting as a mirror the glory
of Christ, are changed into the same image."   Nothing could
have been more simple, more intelligible, more natural, more
supernatural.   It is an analogy from everyday fact.   (1)

February 2   **What's Really Wanted!**

The amount of spiritual longing in the world—in the
hearts of unnumbered thousands of men and women in whom
we would never suspect it; among the wise and thoughtful;
among the young and gay, who seldom assuage and never

betray their thirst—this is one of the most wonderful and touching facts of life. It is not more heat that is needed, but more light; not more force, but a wider direction to be given to very real energies already there. (23)

February 3   **Religious If—**

Many men would be religious if they knew where to begin; many would be more religious if they knew where it would end. It is not indifference that keeps some men from God, but ignorance. "Good Master, what must I do to inherit eternal life?" is still the deepest question of the age. (22)

February 4   **Revolt Against Cant**

These men are in revolt against the kind of religion which we exhibit to the world against the cant that is taught in the name of Christianity. And of the men that have never seen the real thing—if you could show them that, they would receive it as eagerly as you do. They are merely in revolt against the imperfections and inconsistencies of those who represent Christ to the world. (28)

February 5   **The Growing Soul**

To await the growing of a soul is an almost divine act of faith. How pardonable, surely, the impatience of deformity with itself, of a consciously despicable character standing before Christ, wondering, yearning, hungering, to be like that? Yet one must trust the process fearlessly, and without misgiving. "The Lord, the Spirit," will do His part. (1)

February 6   **Religion No Added Thing**

We hear much of love to God. Christ spoke much of love to man. We make a great deal of peace with heaven. Christ made much of peace on earth. Religion is not a strange or added thing, but the inspiration of the secular life, the breathing of an eternal spirit through this temporal world. (21)

February 7   **Impaired Instruments**

The instrument with which we attempt to investigate truth is impaired. Some say it fell, and the glass is broken. Some say prejudice, heredity, or sin, have spoiled its sight, and have blinded our eyes and deadened our ears. In any case the instruments with which we work upon truth, even in the strongest men, are feeble and inadequate to their tremendous task.   (28)

February 8   **The Art of Life**

Few men know how to live. We grow up at random, carrying into mature life the merely animal methods and motives which we had as little children. And it does not occur to us that all this must be changed; that much of it must be reversed; that life is the finest of the Fine Arts; that it has to be learned with life-long patience, and that the years of our pilgrimage are all too short to master it triumphantly. Yet this is what Christianity is for—to teach men the Art of Life. And its whole curriculum lies in one word—"Learn of Me." (23)

February 9   **Learning His Art**

Christ never said much in mere words about the Christian Graces. He lived them, He was them. Yet we do not merely copy Him. We learn His art by living with Him, like the old apprentices with their masters.   (42)

February 10   **Christ and Outsiders**

I say that the men who are perplexed—the men who come to you with serious and honest difficulties—are the best men. They are men of intellectual honesty, and cannot allow themselves to be put to rest by words, by phrases, or traditions, or theologies, but who must get to the bottom of things for themselves. And if I am not mistaken, Christ was very fond of these men. The outsiders always interested Him, and touched Him. The orthodox people—the Pharisees—He was much less interested in. He went with publicans and sinners—with people who were in revolt against the respectability, intellectual and religious, of His day.   And following Him, we are entitled to give sympathetic consideration to those whom He loved and took trouble with.   (28)

February 11   **What about Evolution?**
How am I to reconcile my religion, or any religion, with the doctrine of evolution?   That upsets more men than perhaps anything else at the present hour.   How would you deal with it?   I would say this to a man that Christianity is the further evolution, the higher evolution, pushes the man farther on. It takes him where nature has left him, and carries him on to heights which on the plain of nature he could never reach. That is evolution.   "Lead me to the Rock that is higher than I."   That is evolution.   It is the development of the whole man in the highest directions—that drawing out of his spiritual being.   (28)

February 12   **Adding Life to Life**
Well, if God can give life, He can surely add life. Regeneration is nothing in principle but the adding of more life.   It is God adding life to life—more life to a man who has some life.   (6)

February 13   **Evolution and Theology**
The supreme contribution of Evolution to Religion is that it has given it a clearer Bible.   Science is the great explainer, the great expositor, not only of nature, but of everything it touches.   Its function is to arrange things and make them reasonable.   Evolution has given to theology some wholly new departments.   It has given to it a vastly more reasonable body of truth about God and man, about sin and salvation.   It has lent it a firmer base, an enlarged horizon, and a wider faith. (20)

February 14   **God's Character**
When God told His people His name He simply gave them His character, His character which was Himself; "And the

Lord proclaimed the Name of the Lord . . . the Lord God, merciful and gracious, long-suffering and abundant in goodness and truth. (27)

February 15   Life's Opportunities
Is life not full of opportunities for learning love? Every man and every woman every day has a thousand of them. The world is not a playground; it is a schoolroom. Life is not a holiday, but an education. And the one eternal lesson for us all is *how better can we love?* (21)

February 16   Resolving the Problem
The true problem of the spiritual life may be said to be, do the opposite of neglect. It will just mean that you are so to cultivate the soul that all its powers will open out to God, and in beholding God be drawn away from sin. (22)

February 17   A Living Sacrifice
It is well to remember that we are to give our bodies a living sacrifice—not a half-dead sacrifice, as some people seem to imagine. (25)

February 18   Imitation v Reflection
Imitation is mechanical, reflection organic. The one is occasional, the other organic. In the one case man comes to God and imitates Him; in the other, God comes to man and imprints Himself upon him. (1)

February 19   Mother-Brother-Sister
The first thing a baby needs who comes into the world and begins to live is food. I searched my Bible for food for the ideal man, and found it: "My meat is to do the will of Him who sent Me." After a child has found food, the next thing needed is companionship. The hunger of the affections begins to speak, and the child begins to feel around after objects of affection . . . "Whosoever doeth the will of My Father which is in heaven, the same is My mother, my sister and brother."

All the people in the world, black and white, rich and poor, educated and illiterate, who are doing the will of God, are my mother, my brother, and my sister. (7)

February 20 **The Kingdom as Leaven**

Christ likened the kingdom of God to leaven, and one cannot get a better understanding of the meaning of this phrase than by taking His own metaphor. Christ saw that the world was sunken and that it had to be raised. Leaven comes from the same word as lever does, that which lifts or raises, and Christ founded a Society of men for the purpose of raising the world. The kingdom of God is like leaven. (9)

February 21 **Winning Influence**

The Christian man, simply by virtue of the life that is in him—not by attempting much in the way of forcing it upon others—but by his own spontaneous nature can so work upon men that they cannot but feel that he has been with Jesus. When they look through him and perceive the fragrance of his spirit and the Christlikeness of his life, they remember Christ—they are reminded of Christ by him; and a longing comes over them to live like that, and breathe that air and have that calm, that meekness and that beauty of character; and by that unconscious influence going out as a contagious power, men are won to Christ, and by these men the world is raised. (9)

February 22 **When to Repent**

All the world are at one with Peter in his sin; but not all the world are one with him in his penitence . . . Peter's penitence came sharp upon his sin. It was not on his death-bed nor in his after-life, but just when he had sinned. (6)

February 23 **The Saving Gift**

If you will not receive Salvation as a fact, receive the Lord Jesus Christ as a gift—we ask no questions about a gift. Receive the Lord Jesus Christ as a gift, and thou shalt be saved from the power and the stain and the guilt of Sin, for His is the power and the glory. Amen. (6)

February 24   **Addition to Perfection**

Do not quarrel therefore with your lot in life. Do not complain of its never-ceasing cares, its petty environment, the vexations you have to stand, the small and sordid souls you have to live and work with. Above all, do not resent temptation; do not be perplexed because it seems to thicken round you more and more, and ceases neither for effort nor for agony nor prayer. That is your practice. That is the practice which God appoints you; and it is having its work in making you patient, and humble, and generous, and unselfish, and kind, and courteous. Do not grudge the hand that is mouldering the still too shapeless image within you. It is growing more beautiful, though you see it not, and every touch of temptation may add to its perfection.   (21)

February 25   **Compulsive Reading**

Go home and read the four little books which tell you about His life. Take Matthew, for instance, and if you don't run aground in the 5th chapter and find yourself compelled to spend a week over it, you haven't much moral nature left . . . I have known men who have tried that experiment, who have begun to read the gospel of Matthew, and by the time they had finished reading the 5th chapter, they had thrown in their lot with the Person who forms the subject of that book.   (11)

February 26   **An Obvious Stain**

Society is not wise enough to see the power of sin, or religious enough to see the guilt of sin; but it cannot fail to see the stain of it.   (6)

February 27   **In Temptation's Hour**

Religion is not a blue ribbon to wear against a single set of things. It is not an inoculation against a single disease. A man must accept Christ all around, not only as his Deliverer from sin, but as his friend and guide, his ideal and Saviour . . . He must walk his whole life, and every day of his life, not merely rushing into the top story when temptations are at his heels but dwelling there, in that place where the air is always sweet, where the company is always pure, and where there is nothing to hinder the soul from communing with God and the stars. If a man can continuously live in that region, he is bound to grow better and better. (15)

February 28   **The Deepest Questions**
The questions which conscience sends up to us are always the deepest questions. And the man who has never sent the question, "Where can I get pardon?" has never been into his conscience to find the deepest want he has. It is not enough for him to look lifeward; he must look Godward. And it is not enough to discover the stain of his past, and cry out, "I have sinned." But he must see the guilt of his life and cry, "I have sinned *against God*." (6)

February 29   **Hope of Heaven**
Whatever hopes of a "heaven" a neglected soul may have, can be shown to be an ignorant and delusive dream. How is the soul to escape to heaven if it has neglected for a lifetime the means of escape from the world and self? And where is the capacity for heaven to come from if it be not developed on earth? (22)

March 1   **The Great Phrase**
The great phrase that was never off Christ's lips was the "kingdom of God." It was by far the commonest phrase in His teaching. Have you ever given a month of your life to finding out what Christ meant by the kingdom of God? (9)

March 2   **Destructive Power**
There is something in every man's life which he needs saving from, something which would spoil his life and run off with it into destruction if let alone. This principle of destruction is the first great fact of sin—its *power*. (6)

March 3   Religious Cultivation

"Talent forms in solitude," says the German poet; "character amidst the storms of life." And if religious character is developed and strengthened in the battle of the world, it is no less true that religious talents are cultivated in quiet contemplation and communion with God alone. (6)

March 4   Holiness

Holiness is an infinite compassion for others: Greatness is to take the common things of life and walk truly among them: Happiness is a great love and much serving. (14)

March 5   God in Career

The great reason possibly why so few have thought of taking God into their career is that so few have really taken God into their life. No one ever thinks of having God in his career, or need think, until his life is fully moulded into God's. And no one will succeed in knowing even what God in his career can mean till he knows what it is to have God in the secret chambers of his heart. (6)

March 6   Think and Marvel Not

Think of Bunyan the sinner, think of Newton the miscreant, think of Saul the persecutor, and marvel not, as if it were impossible that a man should be born again. (6)

March 7   Conversion is Personal

Personal conversion means for life a personal religion, a personal trust in God, a personal debt to Christ, a personal dedication to His cause. (27)

March 8   Pursuit of Holiness

When shall we learn that the pursuit of holiness is simply the pursuit of Christ? Sanctity is in character, and not in moods. Divinity in our own plain, calm humanity, and in no mystic rapture of the soul. (1)

March 9   **Reflected Light**

If you cannot at once and always feel the play of His life upon yours, watch for it indirectly. Christ is the Light of the world, and much of His Light is reflected from things in the world—even from clouds.   (12)

March 10   **Work Out Salvation**

Each man in the silence of his own soul must work out this salvation for himself with fear and trembling—with fear, realising the momentous issue of his task; with trembling, lest before the tardy work be done the voice of death should summon him to sleep.   (22)

March 11   **If You Love**

In those days men were working their passage by keeping the Ten Commandments, and the hundred and ten other commandments which they had manufactured out of them. Christ said, I will show you a more simple way. If you do one thing you will do these hundred and ten things without ever thinking about them. If you *love* you will unconsciously fulfil the whole law.   (21)

March 12   **Not Resignation**

"Thy will be done." Let us notice that this prayer does not mean resignation: it is not passive, but active. To pray this prayer is not in effect to say, "God is evidently going to have His way and we may just as well succumb; it is of no use to kick against the pricks; let us just resign at once; Thy will be done." It is an active prayer, and means, "Let that will work through the earth; let it be done in the world; let it be as energetic in the world, as it is triumphant in heaven, until it carries and sweeps everything in the earth along with it!" "Thy will be done!"   (7)

March 13   **Prevent Rottenness**

Christ said that the followers of Him are the salt of the earth and it is that salt that helps to take away the rottenness of the world ... Salt is that which keeps things from becoming rotten. You put salt upon meat and salt upon fish to prevent them from being rotten, and it is the Christian men and women in the city and in the country who prevent them from becoming absolutely rotten. It is our duty . . . not only to sweep away rottenness, but to prevent the new generation that is growing up from becoming rotten. (9)

March 14   Regeneration

The essence of Regeneration is a change . . . from an old life to a new one . . . God is no longer avoided, but worshipped; Christ no longer despised, but trusted. (27)

March 15   Deliverance—Only Part of Life

Deliverance from sin is only a part of the Christian life—by no means the whole. It is only one wing of the new nature; but no man can get on with one wing. Deliverance from temptation is only one function of the new nature. Therefore, you must consecrate your whole life to Christianity; and go into it wholly and with a new heart, if you expect to get deliverance in this one direction; and the best way you can do that is to make up your mind that you will give much of your life to Christianity, to purify the air of the world, so that other men will feel less temptation than you do. (16)

March 16   No Isolated Sin!

There is scarcely such a thing as an isolated sin in a man's life. Most sins can be accounted for by what has gone before. Every sin, so to speak, has its own pedigree, and is the result of the accumulated force, which means the accumulated stain of many a preparatory sin. (26)

March 17   Moral Leakage

If only one of the channels of sin be obstructed, experience points to an almost certain overflow through some other part of the nature. Partial conversion is almost always accompanied by such moral leakage; for the pent-up energies accumulate to the bursting-point, and the last state of that soul may be worse than the first. (1)

March 18   Doubt and Unbelief

Christ never failed to distinguish between doubt and unbelief. Doubt is *can't believe;* unbelief is *won't believe.* Doubt is honesty; unbelief is obstinacy. Doubt is looking for light; unbelief is content with darkness. (25)

March 19   God's Calculated Provision

God knew the power of sin in a human soul when He made so great provision. He knew how great it was; He calculated it. Then He sent the living Christ against it. It is the careful and awful estimate of the power of Sin. God saw that nothing else would do. (6)

March 20   You Must Love Him!

You cannot love to order. You can only look at the lovely object, and fall in love with it, and grow into likeness to it. And so look at this perfect character, this perfect life. Look at the great sacrifice as He laid down Himself, all through life, and upon the Cross of Calvary; and you must love Him. And loving Him, you must become like Him. (21)

March 21   Life Simply Stated

To live greatly like Christ is not to agonise daily over details, to make anxious comparisons with what *we* can do and what *He* did, but a much more simple thing. It is to re-echo Christ's word. It is to have that calm, patient, assured spirit, which reduces life simply to this—a going to the Father. (22)

March 22   Salvation Only Comes . . .

The fact of salvation which God has provided to meet the fact of guilt, although it is the most stupendous fact of all, only comes home to a man when he feels a criminal and stands, like a guilty sinner, for pardon at God's bar. (27)

March 23   Think!

Think of living with oneself for ever and ever. Think of having lived, living now, and evermore living only for this.

Consider Him who endured such contradiction of sinners for our sakes, who made Himself of no reputation, who gave up form and comeliness; who humbled Himself and emptied Himself for us. Then look, if we can, with complacency on such a life—

> "I lived for myself, I thought for myself,
> For myself, and none beside,
> Just as if Jesus had never lived,
> As if He had never died."   (6)

March 24   Atonement!

Christ could not die upon the Cross without witnessing to all eternity of the appalling greatness of human guilt . . . The death of Christ, which is the Atonement, reconciles us to God, makes our religion possible, puts us in the way of power which is to come against our Sin and deliver our life from destruction.   (6)

March 25   We Know!

We all know who deserved to die. We all know Who *did* die. We know *we* were not wounded for our transgressions, we were not bruised for our iniquities. But we know Who was. The Lord hath not dealt with us according to our iniquities; but we know with Whom He has. We know Who bare our sins in His own body on the tree—One who had no sins of His own. We know Who was lifted up like the serpent in the wilderness—He who died, the just for the unjust. If we know this, we know the great fact of Salvation.   (6)

March 26   Freedom and Hope

The freedom from guilt, the forgiveness of sins, come from Christ's Cross; the hope of immortality springs from Christ's grave.   (27)

March 27   Bridging The Grave

"He that hath the Son of God hath Life, and he that hath not the Son hath not Life." This, as we take it, defines the correspondence which is to bridge the grave. This is the new clue to the nature of the Life that lies at the back of the spiritual organism. And this is the true solution of the mystery of Eternal Life. (22)

March 28   **Have You Heard?**

Have you heard that there is another life—a life which cannot die, a life which, linked to your own life, will make the past still bright with pardon and the future rich with hope? *This life is in His Son.* (6)

March 29   **The Supreme Thing**

Love should be the supreme thing—because it is going to last; because in the nature of things it is an Eternal Life. It is a thing that we are living now, not what we are going to get when we die; that we shall have a poor chance of getting when we die unless we are living now. (21)

March 30   **Live After Christ**

Live after Christ, in His Spirit, as in His Presence, and it is difficult to think what more you can do. (1)

March 31   **Correspondence with God**

Uninterrupted correspondence with a perfect environment is eternal life according to science. To know God is to "correspond" with God. To correspond with God is to correspond with a Perfect Environment. And the organism which attains to this, in the nature of things, must live forever. (22)

April 1   **Cradle of Eternity**

Life is the cradle of eternity. As the man is to the animal in the slowness of his evolution, so is the spiritual man to the natural man. Foundations which have to bear the weight of an eternal life must be surely laid. Character is to wear forever; who will wonder or grudge that it cannot be developed in a day? (1)

April 2   **Conversion**

Growth is the work of time. But life is not. At one
moment it was dead; the next it lived. This is conversion, the
"passing," as the Bible calls it, "from Death unto Life." (22)

April 3   **A Colourless Hope**

From time to time the taunt is flung at religion that the
future life of Christianity is simply a prolonged existence, an
eternal monotony, a blind and indefinite continuance of being.
The Bible never could commit itself to any such empty plati-
tude, nor could Christianity ever offer to the world a hope so
colourless.   (22)

April 4   **The Changed Life**

As a matter of fact, to live with Christ did produce this
effect. It produced it in the case of Paul. And during Christ's
lifetime the experience was tried in an even more startling
form. A few raw, unspiritual, uninspiring men, were admitted
to the inner circle of His friendship. The change began at
once. Day by day we can almost see the first disciples grow ...
Slowly the spell of Life deepens. Reach after reach of their
nature is overtaken, thawed, subjugated, sanctified . . . they
find themselves, like their Master, going about and doing
good . . . The people who watch them know how well to
account for it—"They have been," they whisper, "with Jesus."
Already even, the mark and seal of His character is upon them—
"They have been with Jesus." . . . Unparalleled phenomenon,
that these poor fishermen should remind other men of Christ!
Stupendous victory and mystery of regeneration that mortal
men should suggest to the world, *God!* (1)

April 5   **A Life for Christ**

In the perspective of Eternity all lives will seem poor, and
small, and lost, and self-condemned beside a life for Christ.
There will be plenty then to gather round the Cross. But
who will do it now? There are plenty of men to die for Him,
there are plenty to spend Eternity with Christ; but where is
the man who will *live* for Christ? (6)

April 6   Sanctification

The solution of the problem of sanctification is compressed into a sentence: reflect the character of Christ and you will become like Christ.   (1)

April 7   Abiding in Christ

The Christian is a new man in Christ Jesus. He is rooted and built up in Christ; he abides in the Vine, and so abiding, not toiling or spinning, brings forth fruit.   (22)

April 8   All Men Are Mirrors

Reflect the character of Christ and you will become like Christ. All men are mirrors—that is the first law on which this formula is based . . . If all these varied reflections from our so-called secret life are patent to the world, how close the writing, how complete the record, within the soul itself?   (1)

April 9   True Companionship

Our companionship with Him, like all true companionship, is a spiritual communion. All friendship, all love, human and divine, is purely spiritual. It was after He was risen that He influenced even the disciples most.   (1)

April 10   Eternal Bounty

God never keeps anything all to Himself. He who so loved the world that He gave His only begotten Son, does He not with Him freely give us all things? His Son is for us, His love is for us, His will is for us. How do we know that it is so for us? Because this is the will of God, even your sanctification.   (6)

April 11   A Fine Inoculation

Christianity is a fine inoculation, a transfusion of healthy blood into an anaemic or poisoned soul. No fever can attack a perfectly sound body; no fever of unrest can disturb a soul which has breathed the air or learned the ways of Christ.   (22)

April 12   **Withholding of Love**

For the withholding of love is the negation of the spirit of Christ, the proof that we never knew Him, that for us He died in vain. It means that He suggested nothing in all our thoughts, that He inspired nothing in all our lives, that we were not once near enough to Him to be seized with the spell of His compassion for the world. (21)

April 13   **The New Kingdom**

Christianity marks the advent of what is simply a new kingdom. It is, in the conception of its Founder, a kingdom for which all adherents must henceforth exclusively live and work, and which opens its gates alone upon those who, having counted the cost, are prepared to follow it if need be to the death. (22)

April 14   **The Potter and the Clay**

The change we have been striving after is not to be produced by any more striving after. It has to be wrought upon us by the moulding of hands beyond our reach . . . As the branch ascends, and the bud bursts, and the fruit reddens under the co-operation of influences from the outside air, so man rises to the higher stature under invisible pressures from without . . . Our failure has been the failure to put ourselves in the way of the impressed forces. There is a clay, and there is a Potter: we have tried to get the clay to mould the clay. (1)

April 15   **Election**

If you will turn up in your Bibles the meaning of "election," you will find that it is connected, not with salvation in the ordinary sense, but with sanctification. "Whom He did foreknow, He also did predestinate to be conformed to the image of His Son." That is what we are selected for, "to be conformed to the image of His Son." (17)

April 16   **Obey Him!**

Obey Him and you must love Him, Abide in Him, and you must obey Him. Cultivate His friendship. (1)

April 17   **No Place So Dark**

Jesus Christ used to come to men just where they were.
There is no place on earth so dark that the light of heaven will
not come to it; and there is no spot of earth where God may
not choose to raise a monument of His love. There is always
room anywhere in the world for a holy thought.   (6)

April 18   **Under His Influence**

"Make Christ your constant companion"—this is what
it practically means for us. Be more and more under His
influence than any other influence. Ten minutes spent in His
society every day, aye, two minutes if it be face to face, and
heart to heart, will make the whole day different.   (1)

April 19   **Life Straight**

Well, I will tell you how to keep your life straight from
this time—how your hunger after righteousness can be met.
If you become a Christian you will lead a straight life. That
is not all. If you become a Christian you will help other men
to lead straight lives.   (11)

April 20   **Not A Side-Track**

Christianity is not a side-track where a few enthusiasts live
impractical lives on impossible ideals. It is the main stream
of history and of science, and the only current set from eternity
for the progress of the world and the perfecting of the human
race.   (27)

April 21   **Joy Is Other's Gain**

Joy lies in mere constant living in Christ's presence, with
all that that implies of peace, of shelter, and of love; partly in
the influence of that Life upon mind and character and will;
and partly in the inspiration to live and work for others, with
all that that brings of self-riddance and Joy in other's gain. (23)

April 22   **Keeping Up Religious Life**
   The religious life needs keeping up just as the other parts
of our life need keeping up.   There is nothing more impossible
than for a man to live a religious life on an hour's work or an
hour's thought a week . . .   And religion does not live in the
pages of the doctrinal books, but in human life—in conflict with
our own temptations, and in the conduct and character of our
fellow-beings.   (11)

April 23   **Part of the Nourishment**
   Be in the company of good books, beautiful pictures, and
charming, delightful and inspiring music; and let all that one
hears, sees, reads and thinks lift and inspire the higher.   The
man who does that is kept above the lower nature.   Many and
many a thing which is not directly religious, therefore, comes
in to make up a part of the nourishment of the spiritual
life.   (15)

April 24   **Indefinable Love**
   Love itself can never be defined.   Light is something more
than the sum of its ingredients—a glowing, dazzling, tremulous
ether.   And love is something more than all its elements—a
palpitating, quivering, sensitive living thing.   (21)

April 25   **The Meek Possess It**
   The miser does not possess gold; gold possesses him.   But
the meek possess it.   "The meek," said Christ, "inherit the
earth."   They do not buy it; they do not conquer it; but they
inherit it.   (23)

April 26   **Development Begins**
   When a man becomes a Christian the natural process is
this: the Living Christ enters into his soul.   Development
begins.   The quickening life seizes upon the soul, assimilates
surrounding elements, and begins to fashion it . . .   This
fashioning takes a specific form.   It is that of the artist who
fashions.   And all through life this wonderful, mystical,
glorious, yet perfectly definite, process goes on, "until Christ
be formed" in it.   (22)

April 27   **The Noblest Words**

Christianity possesses the noblest words in the language; its literature overflows with terms expressive of the greatest and happiest moods which can free the soul of man—Rest, Joy, Peace, Faith, Love, Light.   (23)

April 28   **"Thy Will Be Done"**

"Thy will be done." He who makes this prayer the prayer of his life will know that of all prayer it is the most truly blessed, the most nearly in the spirit of Him who sought not His own will, but the will of Him that sent Him.   (7)

April 29   **When Life Is Over**

When life is all over, nothing greater can be said of any man than that he did the will of God, whatever that was.   (7)

April 30   **In Saving Men**

In saving men it is very often a life for a life; you have to give your life to the men whom you are trying to better. About the least Christian act a man can do for his brother-man is to talk about Christianity; the case is of a man laying down his life as Christ laid down His life.   (9)

May 1   **Principle of Atonement**

Perhaps he meant to tell us that the principle of the Atonement was a law of Nature . . . that up and down the whole of God's creation the one law of life, the supreme condition of progress, the sole hope of the future is Christ's law of the sacrifice of self.   (19)

May 2   **Happiness—No Mystery**

There is no mystery about Happiness whatever. Put in the right ingredients and it must come out. He that abideth in Him will bring forth much fruit; and bringing forth much fruit is Happiness.   (23)

May 3   **What Is Certain**

We know but little now about the conditions of the life that is to come. But what is certain is that love must last.   (21)

May 4   **To Have Lived With . . .**

To have lived with Socrates—with veiled face—must have made one wise; with Aristides, just.   Francis of Assisi must have made one gentle; Savonarola, strong.   But to have lived with Christ?   To have lived with Christ must have made one like Christ; that is to say, *A Christian.*   (1)

May 5   **Reduce Correspondences**

If a Christian is to "live unto God," he must "die unto sin."   If he does not kill sin, sin will inevitably kill him.   Recognising this, he must set himself to reduce the number of his correspondences—retaining and developing those which lead to a fuller life, unconditionally withdrawing those which in a way tend in an opposite direction.   (22)

May 6   **Never Offer . . . Tell Men!**

The Gospel offers a man life.   Never offer men a thimbleful of Gospel.   Do not offer them merely peace, or merely rest, or merely safety; tell them how Christ came to give men a more abundant life than they have—a life abundant in love, and therefore abundant in salvation for themselves and large in enterprise for the alleviation and redemption of the world.   (21)

May 7   **Standing Idly By**

No one who knows the content of Christianity, or feels the universal need of a religion, can stand idly by while the intellect of his age is slowly divorcing itself from it.   (22)

May 8   **We Know the Best**

I fancy we know pretty well that this is the best purpose to which we can put our life—to do the will of God, and our lives cannot fail as long as we do that.   George Eliot says, "I know no failure save failure in cleaving to the purposes which I know to be the best."   (7)

May 9   **The Highest Ambition**

A man becomes a little attracted to Christ. That grows and grows, into a brighter friendship, and that grows into a great passion, and the man gives himself to Christ's interest, he counts it the highest ambition he can to become a man such as Christ was. You see there is nothing profound about a religion like that.   (11)

May 10   **It Survives Death**

The correspondence of the spiritual man possesses the supernatural virtues of the Resurrection and the Life. Here is a relation established with eternity. The passing years lay no limiting hand on it. Corruption injures it not. It survives death. It, and it only, will stretch beyond the grave, and be found inviolate—

"When the moon is old,
  And the stars grow cold,
  And the books of the Judgment-Day unfold."   (22)

May 11   **The Working Basis**

As Christ's friends, His followers are supposed to know what He wants done, and for the same reason they will try to do it—this is the whole working basis of Christianity.   (27)

May 12   **Beginning to Strike Men**

The fact that Christ led no army, that He wrote no book, built no church, spent no money, but that He loved, and so conquered, this is beginning to strike men.   (6)

May 13   **Life Lost Indeed!**

You are placed where you are, to help on *there* the kingdom of God. You cannot do that when you are old and ready to die. By that time your companions will have fought their fight, and lost or won. If they lose, will you not be sorry that you did not help them? Will you not regret that only at the last you helped the Kingdom of God? Perhaps you will not be able to do it then. And then your life has been lost indeed!   (24)

May 14   **Save Your Lives**

We say nothing to those men about saving their souls.
We say to them: "Gentlemen, save your lives. Do something
with your life. Let that energy, that talent, go out to some
purpose. The world needs the knowledge you have, the
impulses you can give; aye, and the criticisms that you can offer
upon the religious forms about you. It needs all these things.
Save your lives. Do something with them."   (16)

May 15   **Every Atom Can Act**

Every atom in the universe can act on every other atom,
but only through the atom next it. And if a man would act
upon every other man, he can do so best by acting, one at a
time, upon those beside him.   (12)

May 16   **Impress and Reflection**

You can take nothing greater to the heathen world than
the impress and reflection of the Love of God upon your own
character. That is the universal language, that language of
Love, understood by all. It is the man who is the missionary,
it is not his words. His character is his message.   (21)

May 17   **Puzzled?**

I know that many of you are puzzled to know in what
direction you can start to help Christ. "My meat and My
drink," Christ said, "is to do the will of Him that sent Me,"
and if you make up your mind that you are going to do the
will of God above everything else, it matters little in what
direction you work.   (9)

May 18   **Life-Plan Has Choice**

God has a life-plan for every human life. In the eternal
counsels of His will, when He arranged the destiny of every
star, and every sand-grain and every grass-blade, and each of
those tiny insects which live but for an hour, the Creator had a
thought for you and me. Our life was to be the slow unfolding

of this thought, as the corn-stalk from the grain of corn, or the flower from the gradually opening bud. It was a thought of what we were to be, of what we might become, of our influence and our lives. But we all had the terrible power to evade this thought, and shape our lives from another thought, from another will, if we chose. (6)

May 19   **Unconnected with Dullness**
There is no connection between Christianity and a dull life. It is the want of Christianity that makes any life dull. (16)

May 20   **Hopeless Caricatures**
But let us be quite sure when we speak of Christianity that we mean Christ's Christianity. Other versions are either caricatures, or exaggerations, or misunderstandings, or short-sightedness and surface readings. For the most part their attainment is hopeless and the results wretched. (23)

May 21   **Get the Facts!**
The great god of science at the present time is a fact. It works with facts. Its cry is, "Give me facts." Found anything you like upon facts and we will believe you. The spirit of Christ was the scientific spirit. He founded His religion upon facts; and He asked all men to found their religion upon facts. Now, gentlemen, get up the facts of Christianity, and take men to the facts. (28)

May 22   **Rest**
It is only when we see what it was in Him that we can know what the word Rest means. It lies not in emotions, or in the absence of emotions. It is not a hallowed feeling that comes over us in church. It is not something that the preacher has in his voice. It is not in nature, or in poetry, or in music— though in all these there is soothing. It is the mind at leisure from itself. It is the perfect poise of the soul; the absolute adjustment of the inward man to the stress of all outward things; the preparedness against every emergency; the stability of assured convictions; the eternal calm of an invulnerable faith; the repose of a heart set deep in God. (23)

May 23   **Self-Sufficiency**

When one attempts to sanctify himself by effort, he is trying to make his boat go by pushing against the mast. He is like a drowning man trying to lift himself out of the water by pulling at the hair of his own head. The one redeeming feature of the self-sufficient method is this—that those who try it, find out almost at once that it will not gain the goal. (1)

May 24   **Slight Seeking**

There are people who go about the world looking for slights, and they are necessarily miserable, for they find them at every turn—especially the imaginary ones. (21)

May 25   **Downward Drag**

If a man find the powers of sin furiously at work within him, dragging his whole life downward to destruction, there is only one way to escape his fate—to take resolute hold of salvation, and be borne by it to the opposite goal. (22)

May 26   **Ascending Character**

We, reflecting as a mirror the character of Christ, are transformed into the same Image from character to character— from a poor character to a better one, from a better one to a little better still, from that to one still more complete, until by slow degrees the Perfect Image is attained. (1)

May 27   **Growing**

All fruits *grow*—whether they grow in soil or in the soul. No man can *make* things grow. He can *get them to grow* by arranging all the circumstances and fulfilling all the conditions. But the growing is done by God. (23)

May 28   **Universal Cry**

The universal language of the human soul has always been, "I perish with hunger." This is what fits it for Christ. There is a grandeur in this cry from the depths which makes its very unhappiness sublime. (22)

May 29   **Infinite Tokens**

Truth in the Bible is a fountain. It is a diffused nutriment, so diffused that no one can put himself off with the form. It is reached, not by thinking, but by doing. It is seen, discerned, not demonstrated. It cannot be bolted whole, but must be slowly absorbed into the system. Its vagueness to the mere intellect, its refusal to be packed into portable phrases, its satisfying unsatisfyingness, its vast atmosphere, its finding of us, its mystical hold of us — these are the tokens of its infinity. (22)

May 30   **Boundless Influence**

If to live with man diluted to the millioneth degree with the virtues of the Highest can exalt and purify the nature, what bounds can be set to the influence of Christ? (1)

May 31   **Best Prescription**

Christ's yoke is simply His secret for the alleviation of human life. His prescription for the best and happiest method of living. (23)

June 1   **Things which Abide**

I have seen almost all the beautiful things God has made; I have enjoyed almost every pleasure that He has planned for man, and yet as I look back I see standing out above all the life that has gone, four or five short experiences when the love of God reflected itself in some poor imitation, some small act of love of mine, and these seem to be the things which alone of all one's life abide. (21)

June 2   **When Religion Wanes**

When the experimental religion of a man, or of a nation, wanes, religion wanes—their idea of God grows indistinct, and that man, community, or nation, becomes infidel. (25)

June 3   **Voice and Echo**

Sometimes when uncertain of a voice from its very loudness, we catch the missing syllable in the echo. In God and Nature we have Voice and Echo. When I hear both I am assured. My sense of hearing does not betray me twice. I recognise the Voice in the Echo, the Echo makes me certain of the Voice: I listen and I know. (22)

June 4   Imperishables

There is a great deal in the world that is delightful and beautiful; there is a great deal in it that is great and engrossing; but it will not last. All that is in the world, the lust of the eye, the lust of the flesh, and the pride of life, are but for a little while. Love not the world therefore. Nothing that it contains is worth the life and consecration of an immortal soul. The immortal soul must give itself up to something that is immortal. And the only immortal things are these, "Now abideth faith, hope, love, but the greatest of these is love." (21)

June 5   Interpenetration

Souls are not made sweet by taking the acid fluids out, but by putting something in—a great Love, a new Spirit, the Spirit of Christ. Christ, the Spirit of Christ, interpenetrating ours, sweetens, purifies, transforms all. This can only eradicate what is wrong, work a chemical change, renovate and regenerate, and rehabilitate the inner man. (21)

June 6   The Eternal Calm

It is only when we see what it was in Him, that we know what the word rest means. The eternal calm of an invulnerable faith; the repose of a heart set deep in God. (23)

June 7   Receipt for Happiness

The infallible receipt for Happiness, then, is to do good, and the infallible receipt for doing good is to abide in Christ. The surest proof that all this is a plain matter of Cause and Effect is that men may try every other conceivable way of finding Happiness, and they will fail. Only the right cause in each case can produce the right effect. (21)

June 8   **Love Defiant**

Paul . . . in his noble eulogy (I Corinthians 13) has given us
the most wonderful and original account of the *summum bonum*.
We may divide it into three parts. In the beginning . . . we
have Love *contrasted*; in the heart of it, we have Love *analysed*;
toward the end, we have Love *defended* as the supreme gift. (21)

June 9   **Morality Limited**

Morality, at the utmost, only develops the character in
one or two directions. It may perfect a single virtue here and
there, but it cannot perfect all.   (22)

June 10   **Summary Suicide!**

Now, the least experience of life will make it evident that
a large class of sins can only be met, as it were, by suicide.
The peculiar feature of death by suicide is that it is not only
self-inflicted, but sudden. And there are many sins which
must either be dealt with suddenly, or not at all.   (22)

June 11   **Spiritual Environment**

And what is the spiritual environment? It is God.
Without this, therefore, there is no life, no thought, no energy,
nothing—"without Me ye can do nothing."   (22)

June 12   **Better . . . Than Perish**

Better a little faith dearly won, better launched alone on
the infinite bewilderment of Truth, than perish on the splendid
plenty of the richest creeds.   (22)

June 13   **Parasitism**

The natural life not less than the eternal is the gift of God.
But life in either case is the beginning of growth, and not the
end of grace. To pause where we should begin, to retrograde
where we should advance, to seek a mechanical security that
we may cover inertia and find a wholesale salvation in which
there is no personal sanctification—this is Parasitism.   (22)

June 14   **A Balanced Life**

To seize continuously the opportunity of more and more perfect adjustment to better and higher conditions, to balance some inward evil with some purer influence acting from without —these are the secrets of a well-ordered and successful life. (22)

June 15   **Marked Difference**

However active the intellectual or moral life may be, from the point of view of this other life it is dead. That which is flesh is flesh. It wants, that is to say, the kind of life which constitutes the difference between the Christian and the not-a-Christian. It has not yet been "born of the Spirit." (22)

June 16   **Christ's Verdict**

It is the deliberate verdict of the Lord Jesus that it is better not to live than not to love. (21)

June 17   **Complementary!**

The natural life owes all to environment; so must the spiritual. Now, the environment of the spiritual life is God. As nature, therefore, forms the complement of the natural life, God is the complement of the spiritual. (22)

June 18   **Acknowledged**

Believers and unbelievers have been compelled to acknowledge that Christianity holds up to the world the missing type, the perfect men. (22)

June 19   **The True Discovery**

The true discovery of a character is the discovery of its ideals. Paul spares us any speculation in his case. "To me to live," he says, "is Christ." This is the motto of his life, the ruling passion of it, which at once explains the nature of his success and accounts for it. He lives for Christ. (6)

June 20   **Enthusiastic Religion**

An enthusiastic religion is the perfection of common sense. And to be beside oneself for Christ's sake is to be beside Christ, which is man's chief end for time and eternity.   (6)

June 21   **Kept Out!**

How many prodigals are kept out of the Kingdom of God by the unlovely characters of those who profess to be inside!   (21)

June 22   **Accept The Facts**

Then, as I have already said, creeds are human versions of Divine truths; and we do not ask a man to accept all the creeds, any more than we ask him to accept all Christians. We ask him to accept Christ, and the facts about Christ, and the words of Christ.   (28)

June 23   **Why Stumble?**

One can never evacuate life of mysticism. Home is full of it, love is full of it, religion is full of it. Why stumble at that in the relation of man to Christ which is natural in the relation of man to man?   (1)

June 24   **Delights of Life**

I would not rob a man of his problems, nor would I have another man rob me of my problems. They are the delight of life, and the whole intellectual world would be stale and unprofitable if we knew everything.   (25)

June 25   **Remove the Cap!**

There is a little preliminary that the astronomer has to do before he can make his observation. He has to take the cap off his telescope. Many a man thinks he is looking at truth when he is only looking at the cap.   (25)

June 26   **Science Dooms Atheism**

It is a remarkable thing that after trailing its black length for centuries across European thought, atheism should have had its doom pronounced by science. With its most penetrating gaze science has now looked at the back of phenomena. It says: "The atheist tells us there is nothing there. We cannot believe him. We cannot tell what it is, but there is certainly something. Agnostics we may be, we can no longer be atheists." (20)

June 27   **Solemn Moment Reached**

It is a solemn moment when the slow-moving mind reaches at length the verge of its mental horizon and, looking over, sees nothing more. Its straining makes the abyss but more profound. Its cry comes back without an echo. Where is the environment to complete this rational soul? Men either find one—*One*—or spend the rest of their days in trying to shut their eyes. (22)

June 28   **Coarse Treatment**

Coarse treatment never wins souls. So God did not drive the chariot of His omnipotence up to Peter and command him to repent. God did not threaten him with thunderbolts of punishment. God did not even speak to him. That one look laid a spell upon his soul which was more than voice or language through all his after-life. (27)

June 29   **Christ's Religion**

Christ's life was His religion: each day as it came brought round in the ordinary course its natural ministry. Each village along the highway had someone waiting to be helped. (27)

June 30   **Unanswered Prayer**

Thousands of prayers are never answered, simply because God does not wish them. If we pray for any one thing, or any number of things we are sure God wishes, we may be sure our wishes will be gratified. For our wishes are only the reflection of God's. (6)

July 1   **Same Kind of World**
Living in the spiritual world is just as simple as living in
the natural world; and it is the same kind of simplicity, for it
is the same kind of world—there are not two kinds of
world.   (22)

July 2   **The Same Absurdity**
Why a virtuous man should not simply grow better and
better, until in his own right he enter the kingdom of God, is
what thousands honestly and seriously fail to understand. But
if it be simply pointed out that this is the same absurdity as to
ask why a stone should not grow more and more living, till it
enters the organic world, the point is clear in an instant.   (22)

July 3   **Vivid Remembrance**
In looking back upon my experience, that part of my
life which stands out, and which I remember most vividly, is
just that part that has had some conscious association with
Christ. All the rest is pale and thin, and lies like clouds on the
horizon.   (1)

July 4   **Faith Secondary!**
We have become accustomed to be told that the greatest
thing in the religious world is faith. That great word has been
the key-note for centuries of the popular religion, and we have
easily learned to look upon it as the greatest thing in the world.
Well, we are wrong. "The greatest of these is love."   (21)

July 5   **Not Subtraction**
Banish forever from your minds the idea that religion is
subtraction. It does not tell us to give things up, but rather
gives us something so much better that they give themselves
up.   (24)

July 6   **How Sight Sees**
There is a sense of sight in the religious nature. Neglect
this, leave it undeveloped, and you never miss it. You simply

see nothing. But develop it and you see God. And the line along which to develop it is known to us. Become pure in heart. The pure in heart shall see God. (22)

July 7   To Be Yoked
A yoke is not an instrument of torture; it is an instrument of mercy. It is not a malicious contrivance for making work hard; it is a gentle device to make hard labour light. And yet men speak of the yoke of Christ as if it were a slavery, and look upon those who wear it as objects of compassion. (23)

July 8   Joy Follows Fruit
Fruit first, joy next; the one the cause or medium of the other. Fruit-bearing is the necessary antecedent. Joy both the necessary consequent and the necessary accompaniment. (23)

July 9   Social Progress of Humanity
Let them study the social progress of humanity, the spread of righteousness, the gradual amelioration of life, the freeing of slaves, the elevation of women, the purification of religion, and let them ask what these could be if not the coming of the Kingdom of God on earth. If the Church does not rise to the opportunity, it would be left behind. (27)

July 10   Studying Nature
To watch uninterruptedly the same few yards of universe unfold its complex history; to behold the hourly resurrection of new living things and miss no change or circumstance, even of its minuter parts; to look at all, especially the things you have seen before a hundred times, to do all with patience and reverence—this is the only way to study nature. (26)

July 11   Parasitical Praying
Instead of having learned to pray, the ecclesiastical parasite becomes satisfied with being prayed for. His transactions with the Eternal are effected by commission. His work for Christ is done by a paid deputy. His whole life is a prolonged

indulgence in the bounties of the church, and surely—in some cases at least the crowning irony—he sends for the minister when he lies down to die. (22)

July 12   **Ill-Judged Sneer**

The sneer at the godly man for his imperfections is ill-judged. A blade is a small thing. At first it grows very near the earth. It is often soiled and crushed and down-trodden. But it is a living thing. The great dead stone beside it is more imposing; only it will never be anything else than a stone. But this small blade—*it doth not yet appear what it shall be.* (22)

July 13   **Source of Joy**

Through whatever media it reaches us, all true joy and gladness find their source in Christ. (21)

July 14   **Envy Not!**

Whenever you attempt a good work you will find other men doing the same kind of work, and probably doing it better. Envy them not. Envy is a feeling of ill-will to those who are in the same line as ourselves, a spirit of covetousness and detraction. (21)

July 15   **Unknown—Absurd**

A science without mystery is unknown. A religion without mystery is absurd. (22)

July 16   **Looking at Truth**

Men look at truth, at different bits of it, and they see different things of course, and they are very apt to imagine that the thing which they have seen is the whole affair—the whole thing. In reality, we can only see a very little bit at a time; and we must, I think, learn to believe that other men can see bits of truth as well as ourselves. (25)

July 17   **The Evidence and Triumph**

Just because God worketh in him, as the evidence and triumph of it, the true child of God works out his own salvation —works it out having really received it—not as a light thing, a superfluous labour, but with fear and trembling, as a reasonable and indispensable service.   (22)

July 18   **The Husk**

The temporal is the husk and framework of the eternal, and thoughts can be uttered only through things.   (22)

July 19   **Oneness with God**

The goal of the organisms of the spiritual world is nothing less than this—to be "holy as He is holy, and pure as He is pure." And by the Law of Conformity to Type, their final perfection is secured. The inward nature must develop out according to its type, until the consummation of oneness with God is reached.   (22)

July 20   **Breath of Life**

The breath of God, blowing where it listeth, touches with its mystery of life the dead souls of men; bears them across the bridgeless gulf between the natural and the spiritual, between the spiritually inorganic and the spiritually organic; endows them with its own high qualities, and develops within them these new and secret faculties by which those who are born again are said to see the kingdom of God.   (22)

July 21   **Botany of Christ!**

Earnest souls who are attempting sanctification by struggle, instead of sanctification by faith, might be spared much humili- ation by learning the Botany of the Sermon on the Mount. (38)

July 22   **Misplaced Religion**

Religion out of its place in a human life is the most miserable thing in the world. There is nothing that requires so much to be kept in its place as religion, and its first place is what? Second? Third? "First!"   (22)

July 23   **No Vital Connection**

The recognition of the ideal is the first step in the direction
of conformity. But let it be clearly observed that it is but a
step. There is no vital connection between merely seeing the
idea and being conformed to it. Thousands admire Christ
who have never become Christians.   (22)

July 24   **Faith Shaken**

It is quite erroneous to suppose that science ever overthrows
faith, if by that is implied that any natural truth can oppose
successfully any single spiritual truth. Science cannot overthrow
faith; but it shakes it.   (48)

July 25   **True Hope**

A religion of effortless adoration may be a religion for an
angel, but never for a man. Not in the contemplative, but in
the active, lies true hope; not in rapture, but in the realm of
reality, lies true life; not in the realm of ideals, but among
tangible things, is man's sanctification wrought   (1)

July 26   **Be Still and Know**

If God is adding to our spiritual nature, unfolding the new
nature within us, it is a mistake to keep twitching at the petals
with our coarse fingers . . . If God is spending work upon a
Christian, let him be still and know that it is God. And if he
wants work he will find it there—in the being still.   (22)

July 27   **Restore to New Grace**

It is the beautiful work of Christianity everywhere to
adjust the burdens of life to those who bear it, and them to it.
It has a perfectly miraculous gift of healing. Without doing
any violence to human nature, it sets it right with life, har-
monising it with all surrounding things, and restoring those
who are jaded with the fatigue and dust of the world to a new
grace of living.   (23)

July 28   **In Our House!**

To be a Christian is to have that character (the Founder of
Christianity) for our ideal in life, to live under the influence, to
do what He would wish us to do, to live the kind of life He
would have lived in our house, and had He our day's routine to
go through.   (3)

July 29   **How the Bible Came**

The Bible came out of religion, not religion out of the
Bible . . . The Bible is a product of religion, not the cause of
it . . . The historical books came out of facts; the devotional
books came out of experiences; the letters came out of circumstances; and the Gospels came out of all three. That is where
the Bible came from . . . You see the difference. The religion
is not, then, in the writing alone; but in those facts, experiences,
circumstances, in the history and development of a people led
and taught by God. And it is not the words that are inspired
so much as the men.   (4)

July 30   **God-Given Truth**

Truth is not a product of the intellect alone; it is a product
of the whole nature. The body is engaged in it, and the mind,
and the soul. We can make no progress without the full use
of all the intellectual powers that God has endowed us
with.   (5)

July 31   **Organ of Knowledge**

The organ of knowledge is not nearly so much mind, as
the organ that Christ used, namely, obedience; and that was
the organ which He Himself insisted upon when He said: "He
that willeth to do His will shall know of the doctrine whether
it be of God." . . . It doesn't read, "If any man do His will,"
which no man can do perfectly; but if any man be simply
willing to do His will—if He has an absolutely undivided mind
about it—that man will know what truth is and know what
falsehood is; a stranger will he not follow.   (5)

August 1   **Deaf and Blind**

Christ has made us aware that it is quite possible for a man
to have ears and hear nothing, and to have eyes and see not.
One of the disciples saw a great deal of Christ, and he never
knew Him. "Have I been so long time with you, Philip, and
yet hast thou not known Me?" "He that hath seen Me hath
seen the Father also." Philip had never seen Him.   (5)

August 2   **Sanctified Truth**

And I would just add this one thing more: the test of value
of the different verities of truth depends upon one thing:
whether they have or have not a sanctifying power . . . That is
another remarkable association in the mind of Christ—of
sanctification with truth—thinking and holiness—not to be
found in any of the sciences or in any of the philosophies. It
is peculiar to the Bible. Christ said, "Sanctify them through
Thy truth. Thy Word is Truth." . . . And above all, let us
remember to hold the truth in love. That is the most
sanctifying influence of all.   (5)

August 3   **Man Was Made for This**

With Browning: "I say that Man was made to grow, not
stop." Or, in the deeper words of an older Book: "Whom He
did foreknow, He also did predestinate . . . to be conformed to
the Image of His Son." . . . Under the right conditions it is as
natural for character to become beautiful as for a flower: and
if on God's earth there is not some machinery for effecting it,
the supreme gift to the world has been forgotten. This is
simply what man was made for.   (1)

August 4   **Revolution**

In the new version of the New Testament the word "soul"
is always translated in this connection by the word "life" . . .
That marks a revolution in popular theology, and it will make
a revolution . . . in the country where it comes to be seen that a
man's Christianity does not consist in merely saving his soul,
but in sanctifying and purifying the lives of his fellow-men. (3)

August 5   Scrappy Experience

Our Christian experience is very apt to be made of scraps, bits of sermons, stray texts, and isolated sentences, instead of being of a piece and of increasing forces directed constantly from the beginning of life until the curtain drops. (7)

August 6   Localise It!

All men may be saved; hence the prayer Thy will be done, is followed by the expression, "Thy kingdom come." Let us localise that prayer; let us localise it and particularise it and get it into the bit of the world that we are responsible for and not lose it in space—"Thy will be done!" (7)

August 7   Not By Logic

Long, long ago, God made matter, then He made the flowers and trees and animals, then He made man. Did He stop? Is God dead? If He lives and acts what is He doing? He is making man better. He is carrying on the development of men. It is God which "'worketh in you." The buds of our nature are not all out yet; the sap to make them bloom comes from the God who made us, from the indwelling Christ. Our bodies are the temples of the Holy Spirit, and we must bear this in mind because the sense of God is kept up not by logic, but by experience—we must try to keep alive this sense of God. (9)

August 8   Test of Theology

For it is only a living spirit of truth that can touch dead spirit, and the test of any theology is not that it is logically clear or even intellectually solid, but that it carries with it some sanctifying power. (10)

August 9   Universal Currency

God, the Eternal God, is Love. Covet therefore that everlasting gift, that one which it is certain is going to stand, that one coinage which will be current in the Universe when all other coinages of all the nations of the world shall be useless and unhonoured. You will give yourself to many things, give yourself first to Love. (21)

August 10   **The Separate Kingdom**

Christianity is the infusion into the spiritual man of a new life, of a quality unlike anything else in nature. This constitutes the separate kingdom of Christ, and gives to Christianity alone, of all the religions of mankind, the strange mark of divinity.   (22)

August 11   **The Grower Is The Spirit**

No man can *make* things grow. He can *get them to grow* by arranging all the circumstances and fulfilling all the conditions. But the growing is done by God. Causes and effects are eternal arrangements, set in the constitution of the world; fixed beyond man's ordering. What a man can do is to place himself in the midst of a chain of consequences. Thus he can get things to grow: thus he himself can grow. But the grower is the Spirit of God.   (23)

August 12   **Spectrum of Love**

The Spectrum of Love has nine ingredients:—Patience; Kindness; Generosity; Humility; Courtesy; Unselfishness; Good Temper; Guilelessness; Sincerity—these make up the supreme gift, the stature of the perfect man. You will notice that all are in relation to the known today and the near tomorrow, and not to the unknown eternity.   (21)

August 13   **Lifeless!**

The natural man belongs essentially to this present order of things. He is endowed simply with a high quality of the natural animal life. But it is life of so poor a quality that it is not life at all. He that hath not the Son *hath not life.*   (22)

August 14   **Parasitic Interest**

Our churches overflow with members who are mere consumers. Their interest in religion is purely parasitic. Their only spiritual exercise is the automatic one of inhibition, the clergyman being depended on every Sunday for at least a week's supply.   (22)

August 15   **The Essential Difference**

What, then, is the deeper distinction drawn by Christianity? What is the essential difference between the Christian and the not-a-Christian, between the spiritual beauty and the moral beauty? It is the distinction between the organic and the inorganic. Moral beauty is the product of the natural man, spiritual beauty of the spiritual man.   (22)

August 16   **Always Unexplored Regions**

The elimination of mystery from the universe is the elimination of religion. However far the scientific method may penetrate the spiritual world, there will always remain a region to be explored by a scientific faith.   (22)

August 17   **All Law Is Divine**

Try to give up the idea that religion comes to us by chance, by mystery, or by caprice. It comes to us by natural law, or by supernatural law; for all law is divine.   (21)

August 18   **Touch Called Faith**

And there is a sense of touch to be acquired, such a sense as the woman had who touched the hem of Christ's garment. That wonderful electric touch called faith, which moves the very heart of God.   (22)

August 19   **To Learn Christianity**

To learn arithmetic at fifty is difficult—much more to learn Christianity. To learn simply what it is to be meek and lowly, in the case of one who has had no lessons in that in childhood, may cost him half of what he values most on earth. (23)

August 20   **Their Presence Elevates**

There are some men and some women in whose company we are always at our best. While with them we cannot think mean thoughts or speak ungenerous words. Their mere presence is elevation, purification, sanctity. All the best stops in our nature are drawn out by their intercourse, and we find a music in our souls that was never there before.   (1)

August 21   **Evolution's Demand**

Instead of abolishing a Creative Hand, evolution demands it. Instead of being opposed to Creation, all theories begin by assuming it. (29)

August 22   **Learning to Rest**

Christ says we are to achieve Rest by learning. Now consider the extraordinary originality of this utterance. The last thing most of us would have thought of would have been to associate *Rest* with *Work*. (23)

August 23   **Man's Oldest Theme**

The infinite desirability, the infinite difficulty of being good—the theme is as old as humanity. The man does not live from whose deeper being the same confession has not risen, or who would not give his all tomorrow if he could "close with the offer of becoming a better man." (1)

August 24   **The Law of Influence**

It is the law of influence that we become like those whom we habitually admire. Men are all mosaics of other men. (1)

August 25   **Limits of the Spiritual**

But who is to define the limits of the spiritual? Even now it is very beautiful. Even as an embryo it contains some prophecy of its future glory. But the point to mark is that *it doth not yet appear what it shall be.* (22)

August 26   **Whoever Heard . . . ?**

Whoever heard of gluttony doing God's will, or laziness, or uncleanness, or the man who was careless and wanton of natural life? (6)

August 27   **To Know God's Will**

To *know* God's will, it is as much as to say, *do* God's will.
But how are we to *do* God's will *until* we know it? To *know* it;
that is the very dilemma we are in. And it seems no way out
of it to say, *Do* it and you shall *know* it. We want to know it,
in order to do it; and now we are told to do it, in order to know
it! If any man *do*, he shall *know*.   (6)

August 28   **The True Education**

This is the true education. Teach me to do Thy will.
This was the education of Christ. Wisdom is a great study,
and truth, and good works, and love, and trust, but there is an
earlier lesson—obedience. So the ideal pupil prays, "Teach
me to do Thy will."   (6)

August 29   **Fruit and Some Lives**

Men may not know how fruits grow, but they do know
that they cannot grow in five minutes. Some lives have not
even a stalk on which fruits could hang, even if they did grow
in five minutes. Some have never planted one sound seed of
joy in all their lives; and others, who may have planted a germ
or two, have lived so little in sunshine that they never could
come to maturity.   (23)

August 30   **Living in Glass Houses**

Whether we like it or not, we live in glass houses. The
mind, the memory, the soul, is simply a vast chamber panelled
with looking-glass. And upon this miraculous arrangement
and endowment depends the capacity of mortal souls to "reflect
the character of the Lord."   (1)

August 31   **Spiritually Dead**

The soul which has no correspondence with the spiritual
environment is spiritually dead. It may be that it never
possessed the spiritual eye or the spiritual ear, or a heart that
throbbed in response to the love of God. If so, having never

lived, it cannot be said to have died.   But not to have had these correspondences is to be in the state of death.   To the spiritual world, to the Divine environment, it is dead—as a stone which has never lived is dead to the environment of the organic world.   (22)

September 1   A Vast Capacity for God

The soul, in its highest sense, is a vast capacity for God.   It is like a curious chamber added on to being, and somehow involving being; a chamber with elastic and contractile walls, which can be expanded, with God as its guest, illimitably, but which, without God, shrinks and shrivels until every vestige of the Divine is gone, and God's image is left without God's Spirit.   (22)

September 2   Pressure from Without

As the branch ascends, and the bud bursts, and the fruit reddens under the co-operation of influences from the outside air, so man rises to the higher nature under invisible pressure from without.   (1)

September 3   Till Men Can Say of Us

Till men can say of us, "They suffer long and are kind, they are not easily provoked, do not behave themselves unseemly, bear all things, think no evil," we have no chance against the world.   One repulsive Christian will drive away a score of prodigals.   God's love for poor sinners is very wonderful, but God's patience with ill-natured saints is a deeper mystery.   (21)

September 4   Undiscovered Distinction

Many a man goes through life hanging his head with shame and living without his self-respect because he has never discovered the distinction between temptation and sin.   (34)

September 5   **The New Nature**

The new nature is renewed from day to day. Just as the
body is built up, microscopic cell by microscopic cell, so the
new nature is built up by a long series of crucifixions of the old
nature, by taking in food from the higher world and getting
these things built into our nature which work for righteousness
and truth and beauty and purity.   (34)

September 6   **Science and God**

It is quite clear that Science has gone as far as she ever will
on her side of the border. And she has gone a wonderful
length—*towards us*, as I am convinced. The old cry, "How far
Science has wandered away from God (Creator)," will soon be
entirely obsolete; and "How near Science has come to God" will
be the watchword of the most thoughtful and far-seeing.   (14)

September 7   **Some Special Sin**

What do you think keeps young men from becoming
Christians?—Some special sin which they prefer to Christ—I
think some *one* definite sin. In every life, I believe, there is
some one particular sin, outstanding only to oneself, different
in different cases, but always *one* with which the secret history
is woven through and through. This is that which the
unconverted man will not give up for Christ.   (27)

September 8   **Having Counted the Cost**

Then, after counting the cost, if you really mean to go on,
let every fear about consequences, every doubt about the
success of it, every suspicion of failure, vanish. You have all
the powers of heaven at your back, and you *must* succeed.
Make up your mind to this at once, and go forward in the
fullness of truth in God. Do not be frightened at your own
inexperience, nor think how exceptionally "hard" your town
is. It is God who is to do the work, and not you; so you may
safely leave all anxiety in His hands. Above all, do not be
afraid of making mistakes. Everybody makes mistakes; and
the greatest mistake you could make would be not to begin at
all.   (27)

September 9   Our Business
Sin is a kind of bacillus, and it cannot take root in the world unless there is a soil, and it is our business to make the world's soil pure and sanitarily sweet, so that the disease of sin cannot exist. (16)

September 10   Wonderful History
Every Christian has his own wonderful little history to tell; and when it bubbles right out of his heart, with the sole desire to glorify God, and bring sinners to the Cross, no one ever thinks of the blundering and the faltering. (27)

September 11   What Is Evolution?
Up to this time no word has been spoken to reconcile Christianity with Evolution, or Evolution with Christianity. And why? Because the two are one. What is Evolution? A method of creation. What is its object? To make more perfect living beings. Through what does Evolution work? Through love. Through what does Christianity work? Through love. Evolution and Christianity have the same Author, the same end, the same spirit. There is no rivalry between these processes. (29)

September 12   Living Epistles
Men find Christ through their fellowmen, and every glimpse they get of Him in them is a direct message from Himself. (14)

September 13   Own Work or Masters?
There are two ways in which a workman regards his work— as his own or his Master's. If it were his own, then to leave it in its prime is a catastrophe, if not a cruel and unfathomable wrong. But if it is his Master's, one looks not backward, but before, putting by the well-worn tools without a sigh, and expecting elsewhere better work to do. (19)

September 14   **Gulfs Filled Up**

If nature is the garment of God, it is woven without seam throughout; if a revelation of God, it is the same yesterday, today, and for ever; if the expression of His will, there is in it no variableness nor shadow of turning. Those who see great gulfs fixed—and we have all begun by seeing them—end by seeing them filled up.   (29)

September 15   **Man Is Not Human**

Man is not human. He reaches his full height only when Love becomes to him the breath of life, the energy of will, the summit of desire. There at last lies all happiness, and goodness, and truth, and divinity.   (29)

September 16   **Providence Cares Less**

For providence cares less for winning causes than that men, whether losing or winning, should be great and true; cares nothing that reforms should drag their course from year to year bewilderingly, but that men and nations, in carrying them out, should find there, education, discipline, unselfishness, and growth in grace.   (27)

September 17   **Who Names The Name**

Every man who names the name of Christ, is to create around him an environment of Christ, so that men shall see the Kingdom of God, and grow up like Christ.   (27)

September 18   **The Eternal Beyond—Here**

The eternal beyond is the eternal here. The street-life, the home-life, the business-like, the city-life, in all the varied range of its activity, are an apprenticeship for the City of God. There is no other apprenticeship for it.   (31)

September 19   **Strengthened Beyond Belief**

Science has made religion a thousand times more thinkable and certain. It had become simply impossible for thinking men and women to be at rest on the old theological standpoint.

The basis of religion was getting very weak. Science and literature, so far from weakening the spiritual part of religion, have strengthened it beyond all belief. (27)

September 20   Insensitiveness to God

It means that nothing in life should be dreaded so much as that the soul should ever lose its sensitiveness to God; that God should ever speak and find the ear just dull enough to miss what He has said; that God should have some active will for some human will to perform, and our heart be not the first in the world to be ready to obey. (6)

September 21   Germ or Crystal?

The whole difference between the Christian and the moralist lies here. The Christian works from the centre, the moralist from the circumference. The one is an organism, in the centre of which is planted by the living God a living germ. The other is a crystal, very beautiful it may be; but only a crystal—it wants the vital principle of growth. (22)

September 22   The Power Will Come

If you want to be saved, breathe the breath of life. And if you cannot breathe, let the groans which cannot be uttered go up to God, and the power will come. For all of us alike, if we but ask shall receive. For God makes surpassing allowances, and He will do unto the least of us exceeding abundantly above all that we ask or think. (6)

September 23   This Steadied Christ

The thing that steadied Christ's life was the thought that He was going to His Father. This one thing gave it unity, and harmony, and success. During His whole life He never forgot His Word for one moment. There is no sermon of His where it does not occur; there is no prayer, however brief, where it is missed . . . "The Great Name" was always hovering on His lips, or bursting out of His heart. (22)

September 24   Only Meetness for Heaven

To move among the people on the common street; to meet them in the market-place on equal terms; to live among them not as saint or monk, but as brother-man with brother-man; to serve God not with form or ritual, but in the free impulse of a soul; to carry on the multitudinous activities of the city—social, commercial, political, philanthropic—in Christ's spirit and for His ends: this is the religion of the Son of Man, and the only meetness for Heaven which has much reality to it.   (31)

September 25   No Worse Fate

No worse fate can befall a man in this world than to live and grow old alone, unloving and unloved. To be lost is to live in an unregenerate condition, loveless and unloved; and to be saved is to love; and he that dwelleth in love dwelleth already in God. For God is love.   (21)

September 26   Evidence for Christianity

The evidence for Christianity is not the Evidences. The evidence for Christianity is *a Christian*. The unit of physics is the atom, of biology the cell, of philosophy the man, of theology the Christian.   (20)

September 27   Obedience

Obedience is the organ of spiritual knowledge. As the eye is the organ of physical sight; the mind of intellectual sight; so the organ of spiritual vision is this strange power, Obedience.   (6)

September 28   Magnetised

Loving Him, you must become like Him. Love begets love. It is a process of induction. Put a piece of iron in the presence of a magnetised body, and that piece of iron for a time becomes magnetised. It is charged with an attractive force in the mere presence of the original force, and as long as you leave the two side by side, they are both magnets alike. (21)

September 29   Ultimate Perfection

The life of the senses, high and low, may perfect itself in nature. Even the life of thought may find a large complement in surrounding things. But the higher thought and the conscience and the religious life can only perfect themselves in God.   (22)

September 30   Prevent and Cure!

The work of salt is preventative as well as curative. We do not half enough emphasise the preventative side of Christian activity; we do not half enough emphasise the making of Christian environment, in which the Christ life shall be possible even in the slums of our great cities. That man is doing the work of Christ who is cleansing these places by building new houses, by giving pure air and pure water, by giving good schools, and by in any way bringing sweetness and light and purity to keep young lives from succumbing to the influences which surround them.   (9)

October 1   Love Is Not a Thing

Love is not a thing of enthusiastic emotion. It is a rich, strong, manly, vigorous expression of the whole round Christian character—the Christlike nature in its fullest development. (21)

October 2   Not a Think World

No one has the right to postpone his *life* for the sake of his thoughts. Why? Because this is a real world, not a *think* world. Treat it as a whole—act.   (27)

October 3   Bad Temper

We are inclined to look upon bad temper as a very harmless weakness . . . a mere infirmity of nature, a family failing, a matter of temperament, not a thing to be taken into serious account in estimating a man's character. No form of vice, not worldliness, not greed of gold, not drunkenness itself, does more to un-Christianise society than evil temper. For embittering life, for breaking up communities, for destroying the most sacred relationships, for devastating homes, for withering up men and women, for taking the bloom off childhood, in short, for sheer gratuitous misery-producing power, this influence stands alone. (21)

October 4   The Words We Shall Hear

It is the Son of *Man* before whom the nations of the world shall be gathered. It is in the presence of *Humanity* that we shall be charged . . . The words which all of us shall one Day hear, sound not of theology but of life, not of churches and saints but of the hungry and the poor, not of creeds and doctrines but of shelter and clothing, not of Bibles and prayer-books but of cups of cold water in the name of Christ. (21)

October 5   Save Your Life

In reality Christ never said, "Save your soul." It is a mistranslation which says that. What He said was, "Save your life." And this is not because the first is nothing, but only because it is so very great a thing that only the second can accomplish it. (32)

October 6   Immoral and Unreal

Whatever rest is provided by Christianity for the children of God, it is certainly never contemplated that it should supersede personal effort. And any rest which ministers to indifference is immoral and unreal—it makes parasites and not men. (22)

October 7   Poorest Idolatry

The irreligious man's correspondences are concentrated upon himself. He worships himself. Self-gratification rather than self-denial; independence rather than submission—these are the rules of life, and this is at once the poorest and the commonest form of idolatry. (22)

October 8   Carry Out Christ's Plan

The Programme for the other life is not out yet. For this world, for these faculties, for his one short life, I know nothing that is offered to man to compare with membership in the Kingdom of God. Among the mysteries which compass the world beyond, none is greater than how there can be in store for man a work more wonderful, a life more God-like than this. If you know anything better, live for it; if not, in the name of God and of Humanity, carry out Christ's plan. (32)

October 9   If We Would Follow

If we would follow the eccentricity of our Master, let it not be in asceticism, in denunciation, in punctilliousness, and scruples about trifles, but in largeness of heart, singleness of eye, true breadth of character, true love to men, and heroism for Christ. (6)

October 10   Neglect Despoils

Neglect does more for the soul than make it miss salvation. It despoils it of its capacity for salvation. Degeneration in the spiritual sphere involves primarily the impairing of the faculties of salvation, and ultimately the loss of them. It really means that the very soul itself becomes piecemeal destroyed, until the very capacity for God and righteousness is gone. (22)

October 11   An Imperfect Element

A heart not quite subdued to God is an imperfect element, in which His will can never live; and the intellect which belongs to such a heart is an imperfect instrument and cannot find God's will unerringly—for God's will is found in regions which obedience only can explore. (6)

October 12   Capital of the Kingdom

Heaven is only the *capital* of the kingdom of God; the Bible is the guide-book to it; the church is only the weekly parade of those who belong to it. If you would turn to the seventeenth chapter of St. Luke, you will find out where the kingdom of God really is. "The Kingdom of God is within you"—within *you*. The kingdom of God is *inside people*. (24)

October 13   Theologies

Theologies—and I am not speaking disrespectfully of theology; theology is as scientific a thing as any other science of facts—but theologies are human versions of Divine truths, and hence the varieties of the versions, and the inconsistencies of them. (28)

October 14   Many Current Gospels

Many of the current Gospels are addressed only to a part of man's nature. They offer peace, not life; faith, not love; justification, not regeneration. And men slip back again from such religion because it has never really held them. It offered no deeper and gladder life-current than the life that was lived before. Surely it stands to reason that only a fuller love can compete with the love of the world. (21)

October 15   Enemies of Preaching

The two greatest enemies of preaching are laziness and tradition . . .(When preaching) . . . We dare not give the people wax fruits, fruits which have never grown. We dare not give them stale fruit, nor unripe fruit, nor fruit with the bloom and fragrance gone. (17)

October 16   Christ's Favourite Words

Have you noticed Christ's favourite words? If you have, you must have been struck by two things—their simplicity and their fewness . . . such words as these: world, life, trust, love. But none of these was the greatest word of Christ. His great word was new to religion. That word was Father. (22)

October 17   Law of All Nature

The entire dependence of the soul upon God is not an exceptional mystery, nor is man's helplessness an arbitrary and unprecedented phenomenon. It is the law of all Nature. (27)

October 18   Useless . . . Unless

To examine ourselves is good, but useless unless we also examine environment. To bewail our weakness is right, but not remedial. The cause must be investigated as well as the result. (22)

October 19   Joy Must Be Grown

Christian experiences are not the work of magic, but come under the law of Cause and Effect. In reality, Joy is as much a matter of Cause and Effect as pain. No one can get Joy by merely asking for it. It is one of the ripest fruits of the Christian life, and, like all fruits, must be grown. (23)

October 20   Begin with His Words

But Christ, so far from resenting or discouraging this relation of Friendship, Himself proposed it. "Abide in Me" was almost His last word to the world. And He partly met the difficulty of those who feel its intangibleness by adding the practical clause, "If ye abide in Me *and My words abide in you.*" Begin with His words. Words can scarcely ever be long impersonal. Christ Himself was a Word, a word made Flesh. Make His words flesh; do them, live them, and you must live Christ. (1)

October 21   Marvel!

Human nature demands Regeneration as if it *were* necessary. No man who knows the human heart or human history will marvel as if it were unnecessary that the world must be born again. Every other conceivable measure has been tried to reform it. Marvel not, as if it were unintelligible . . . impossible . . . unnecessary that ye must be born again. *But marvel if you are. Marvel if you are not. Marvel that you may be today.* (6)

October 22   By Experience: Not Logic

All religious truths are doubtable. There is no absolute proof for any of them. Even that fundamental truth—the existence of God—no man can prove by reason. The ordinary proof for the existence of God involves either an assumption, argument in a circle, or a contradiction. The impression of God is kept up by experience; not by logic.   (28)

October 23   Alike for Soul or Stone

It is as natural for our soul to go downward as for a stone to fall to the ground. Do we ever thank God for redeeming our soul from that?   (27)

October 24   The True Environment

The true environment of the moral life is God. Here conscience wakes. Here kindles love. Duty here becomes heroic, and that righteousness begins to live which alone is to live for ever.   (22)

October 25   Mystery of Being Not

Poetry draws near death, only to hover over it for a moment and withdraw in terror . . . Philosophy finds it among the mysteries of being, the one great mystery of being not.   (27)

October 26   The Close of Life

The close of life, the final step of life, the end of it all, is an eternal life; and all the other lives may be very fine, beautiful and interesting, and in their way useful, but this is eternal life—"He that doeth the will of God abideth for ever." Not an hour of a life lived along that line can be lost, because it is a mere conductor to the eternal, a mere physical means of communicating the spiritual law to this natural world.   (7)

October 27   The Maximum Achievement

So true is it that the end of life is to do God's will, that the possession of this principle makes all the difference between happy and depressed work, because the happiness of life, consists in doing God's will . . . The maximum achievement of any human life, when all is over, is to have done the will of God.   (17)

October 28   **Life—Apart from Christ**

The Christian life is the only life that will ever be completed. Apart from Christ the life of man is a broken pillar, the race of man an unfinished pyramid. One by one in sight of eternity all human ideals fall short; one by one before the open grave all hopes dissolve. (22)

October 29   **Love—And Live On!**

We want to live forever for the same reason that we want to live tomorrow. Why do you want to live tomorrow? It is because there is someone who loves you, and whom you want to see tomorrow, and be with and love back. There is no other reason why we should live on than that we love and are beloved. (21)

October 30   **Death Is Sunrise**

As we watch a life which is going to the Father, we cannot think of night, of gloom, of dusk and sunset. It is Life which is the night and Death is sunrise. (27)

October 31   **Death . . . Means?**

Death . . . means reaching the Father. It is not departure, it is arrival; not sleep, but waking. For life to those who live like Christ is not a funeral procession. It is a triumphal march to the Father. And the entry at the last in God's own chariot is the best hour of all. (27)

November 1   **The Universal Fellowship**

And it is, perhaps, true that without any loss in the feeling of saintly communion with those throughout the world who say "Our Father" with him in their prayers, the more he feels that Christ has all of him to himself, the more he feels that he has Christ all to himself. Christ has died for other men, but in a peculiar sense for him. God has a love for all the world, but a peculiar love for him. God has an interest in all the world, but a peculiar interest in him. This is always the instinct of a near fellowship, and it is true of the universal fellowship of God with His own people. (6)

November 2   The Words Most Used

You can unlock a man's whole life if you watch what *words* he uses most. We have each a small set of words which, though we are scarce aware of it, we always work with, and which really expresses all that we mean by life, or have found out of it. For such words embalm the past for us. They have become ours by a natural selection throughout our career of all that is richest and deepest in our experience. So our vocabulary is our history, and our favourite words are ourselves.   (6)

November 3   No Sleeping Saint!

No man can become a saint in his sleep; and to fulfil the condition required demands a certain amount of prayer and meditation and time, just as improvement in any direction, bodily or mental, requires preparation and care. Address yourself to that one thing; at any cost have this transcendent character exchanged for yours.   You will find as you look back upon your life that the moments that stand out, the moments when you have really lived, are the moments when you have done things in a spirit of love.   (21)

November 4   Exercise the Intellect

It may not be necessary for people in general to sift the doctrines of Christianity for themselves, but it is required of a student, whose business it is to think, to exercise the intellect which God has given him in finding out the truth.   (8)

November 5   Absence of God's Will

Just as the loss of assurance of salvation means absence of peace, and faith, and usefulness, so absence of God's will means miserable Christian life, imperfect Christian character, and impaired Christian usefulness.   (27)

November 6   Statesmen of God

The men who get no stimulus from any visible reward, whose lives pass while the objects for which they toil are still too far away to comfort them; the men who hold aloof from dazzling schemes, and earn the misunderstanding of the crowd because they foresee remoter issues, who even oppose a seeming good because a deeper evil lurks beyond—these are the statesmen of the Kingdom of God. (27)

November 7   There Is Your City
You wish . . . to be a religious man.   Well, be one.   There is your City; begin . . .   How are you to begin?   As Christ did. First He looked at the City; then He wept over it; then He died for it. (27)

November 8   Negation of All Religion
To grow up in complacent belief that God had no business in this great world of human beings except to attend to a few religious people was the negation of all religion. (6)

November 9   The Spiritual Substitute
There will be no eye, no pupil, no retina, no optic nerve in the hereafter, so faith is the spiritual substitute for them which Christ would develop in us by going away. (27)

November 10   Internal Ingredients
"Love suffereth long and is kind; love envieth not; love vaunteth not itself."   Get these ingredients into your life. Then everything that you do is eternal.   It is worth doing.   It is worth giving time to. (21)

November 11   Self-Denial Compensation
No man is called to a life of self-denial for its own sake. It is in order to gain a compensation which, though sometimes difficult to see, is always real and always proportionate. (22)

November 12   Nothing by Chance!
Nothing that happens in this world happens by chance. God is a God of order.   Everything is arranged upon definite

principles, and never at random. The world, even the religious world, is governed by law. Character is governed by law. The Christian experiences are governed by law. Men, forgetting this, expect Rest, Joy, Peace, Faith to drop into their souls from the air like snow or rain. But in point of fact they do not do so; and if they did they would no less have their origin in previous activities and be controlled by natural laws. Rain and snow do drop from the air, but not without a long previous history. They are the mature effects of former causes. Equally so are Rest, and Peace, and Joy. (23)

November 13   **Things Christ Condemned**
It seldom occurs to those who repudiate Christianity because of its narrowness or its impracticalness, its sanctimoniousness or its dullness, that these were the very things which Christ strove against and unweariedly condemned. (27)

November 14   **The Spiritual Life**
The spiritual life is the gift of the Living Spirit. The spiritual man is no mere development of the natural man. He is a new creation born from above. (22)

November 15   **Man Must Make His Lever**
Nature never provides for man's wants in any direction, bodily, mental, or spiritual, in such a form as that he can simply accept her gifts automatically. She puts all the mechanical powers at his disposal—but he must make his lever. (22)

November 16   **The Fraction of a Word**
In the vocabulary of science eternity is only the fraction of a word. It means mere everlastingness. To religion, on the other hand, eternity has little to do with time. To correspond with "the true God and Jesus Christ" is eternal life. (22)

November 17   **Battle for Life's Issues**
Temptation . . . cuts a man off from all his fellowmen; and in the silence of his own heart he finds himself fighting out that battle on which the issues of life hang. (21)

November 18   **Value of Theological Question**

The value of any theological question depends upon whether it has a sanctifying influence. If it has not, don't bother about it. Don't let it disturb your minds until you have exhausted all truths that have sanctification within them. (25)

November 19   **Life's First Great Object**

You will give yourself to many things. Give yourselves first to Love. Hold things in their proportion. Let at least the first great object of our lives be to achieve the character of Christ, which is built round Love. (21)

November 20   **State of Penitence**

We find here four outstanding characteristics of the state of penitence: (1) It is a *divine thing*. It began with God. Peter did not turn. But "the Lord turned and looked upon Peter." (2) It is a *very sensitive thing*. A look did it. "The Lord looked upon Peter." (3) It is a *very intense thing*. "Peter went out and wept bitterly." (4) It is a *very lonely thing*. "Peter went out"— out into the quiet night, to be alone with his sin and God. (6)

November 21   **When God Asks Your Gift**

Do you think God wants your body when He asks you to present it to Him? Do you think it is for His sake that He asks it, that He might be enriched by it? God could make a thousand better with a breath. It is for your sake He asks it. He wants your gift to give you His gift—your gift which was just in the way of His gift. He wants your will out of the way, to make room for His will. You give everything to God. God gives it all back again, and more. (6)

November 22   **Sin Demands Penitence**

Every sin that was ever done demands a bitter repentance. And if there is little emotion in a man's religion, it is because there is little introspection. (6)

November 23   **Our Sanctification**

Our sanctification is not in books, or in noble enthusiasm, or in personal struggles after a better life. It is in the offering of the body of Jesus Christ once for all. Justification is through the blood of Jesus Christ once for all. Sanctification is through the body of Jesus Christ once for all. It is not a thing to be generated in fragments of experience at one time and another— it is already complete in Christ. We have only to put on Christ.   (6)

November 24   **Christ's Confidence in Us**

Every communicant is left by Christ with a solemn responsibility. Christ's confidence in us is unspeakably touching. Christ was sure of us: He felt the world was safe in our hands. He was away, but we would be Christs to it; the Light of the World was gone, but He would light a thousand lights, and leave each of us as one to illuminate one corner of its gloom.   (6)

November 25   **How Shall We Escape?**

How shall we escape if we neglect? The answer is, we cannot. In the nature of things we cannot. We cannot escape any more than a man escape drowning who falls into the sea, and has neglected to learn to swim. In the nature of things he cannot escape—nor can he escape who has neglected the great salvation.   (22)

November 26   **Every Hour a Kingdom**

Every hour a *kingdom* is coming in your heart, in your home, in the world near you, be it a kingdom of darkness or a kingdom of light.   (24)

November 27   **One City**

One city . . . where religion had overflowed the churches and passed into the streets . . . permeating the whole social and commercial life—one such Christian city would seal the redemption of the world.   (27)

November 28   **Causes for His Joy**

When He spoke of His Joy remaining with us, He meant in part that the causes which produced it should continue to act. His followers, that is to say, by *repeating* His life would experience its accompaniments. His Joy, His kind of Joy, would remain with them.   (23)

November 29   **Conditional Promises**

If the Bible is closely looked into, it will probably be found that many of the promises have attached to them a condition— itself not infrequently the best part of the promise. True prayer for any promise is to plead for power to fulfil the condition on which it is offered, and which, being fulfilled, is in that act given.   (20)

November 30   **Religion a Nuisance!**

I have not the slightest doubt that there are many men who are seeking second the Kingdom of God, and their religion is a nuisance to them. It is hard to keep up, and they would get rid of it if they could. The cure is to seek it first, to make it the helm of life. Then only can a man's life go straight, and then only can he fulfil the destiny for which God has put him in the world.   (16)

December 1   **The Soul That Sinneth**

The soul that sinneth "it shall die," not necessarily because God passes sentence of death upon it, but because it cannot help dying. It has neglected "the functions which resist death," and has always been dying. The punishment is in its very nature.   (22)

December 2   **Respect Doubt**

Respect doubt for its origin. It is an inevitable thing. It is not a thing to be crushed. It is part of man as God made him. Heresy is truth in the making, and doubt is the prelude of knowledge.   (25)

December 3   **An Immanent God**

When are we to exchange the terrible far away, absentee
God of our childhood for the everywhere present God of the
Bible? . . . Let us gather together the conception of an
immanent God; that is the theological word for it, Immanuel—
God with us—an inside God, an immanent God.   (8)

December 4   **The Visible Ladder**

The visible is the ladder up to the invisible, the temporal
is but the scaffolding of the eternal. And when the last im-
material souls have climbed through this material to God,
the scaffolding shall be taken down, and the earth dissolved
with fervent heat—not because it was base, but because its
work was done.   (22)

December 5   **Work of a Moment**

While growth is a slow and gradual process, the change
from death to life, alike in the natural and spiritual spheres, is
the work of a moment. Whatever the conscious hour of the
second birth may be—in the case of an adult it is probably
defined by the first real victory over sin—it is certain that on
biological principles the real turning-point is literally a
moment.   (22)

December 6   **The End of Life**

The end of life is simply to do God's will, whether that be
working or waiting, winning or losing, or suffering or recovering,
or living or dying. Death can only be gain when to have lived
was Christ.   (19)

December 7   **Goal of Evolution**

The work begun by nature is finished by the supernatural
—as we are wont to call the higher natural. And as the veil
is lifted by Christianity it strikes men dumb with wonder. For
the goal of evolution is Jesus Christ.   (25)

December 8   **It Will Not Last!**

John says of the world, not that it is wrong, but simply
that "it passeth away." There is a great deal in the world that
is delightful and beautiful; there is a great deal in it that is
great and engrossing; but it will not last.   (21)

December 9   **Judged by Nature Now**

Every soul is a Book of Judgment, and Nature, as a recording
angel, marks there every sin. As all will be judged by the
great Judge some day, all are judged by Nature now. The
sin of yesterday, as part of its penalty, has the sin of today. All
follow us in silent retribution on our past, and go with us to the
grave.   (22)

December 10   **The Educated Eye**

The discipline of life is a preparation for meeting the
Father. When we arrive there to behold His beauty, we must
have the educated eye; and that must be trained here. We
must become so pure in heart—and it needs much practice—
that we shall see God. That explains life—why God puts man
in the crucible and makes him pure by fire.   (22)

December 11   **The Bible Does Not Say**

The Bible does not say that everybody who is not a Christian
is a notorious sinner; but it says that the man who lives outside
that is wasting his life. He may not be doing wrong, but his
life is lost.   (11)

December 12   **Christ in You**

The passage from the Natural World to the Spiritual
World is hermetically sealed on the natural side. No organic
change, no modification of environment, no mental energy, no
moral effort, no evolution of character, no progress of civilisa-
tion. can endow any single human soul with the attributes of

Spiritual Life . . . Christianity is the infusion into the spiritual man of a new life, of a quality unlike anything else in nature. Revelation names it—"Christ in you." "I am in the Father, ye in Me and I in you" (John 14: 20). (22)

December 13   Training for Eternity
Trial to the Christian is training for eternity, and he is perfectly contented; for he knows that "he who loveth his life in this world shall lose it; but he that hateth his life in this world shall keep it unto life eternal." He is keeping his life till he gets to the Father. (22)

December 14   Only Use of Truth
The only use of truth is its sanctifying power; and that is the peculiarity of the truth of Christianity, that it has this sanctifying power and makes men better. (11)

December 15   No Middle Way
There is no middle way in religion—self or Christ. The quality of the selfishness—intellectual, literary, artistic— the fact that our self's centre may be of a superior order of self, does nothing to destroy this grave distinction. It lies between self and Christ. (Hebrews 12: 2.) (27)

December 16   Splendour of Salvation
Mark well also the splendour of this idea of salvation. It is not merely final "safety," to be forgiven sin, to evade the curse. It is not vaguely, "to get to heaven." It is to be conformed to the Image of the Son. It is for these poor elements to attain to the Supreme Beauty. (22)

December 17   No Small Sin
There is such a thing in the world as a great sin, but there is no such thing as a small sin. The smallest sin is a fall, and a fall is a fall from God, and to fall from God is to fall the greatest height in the universe. (6)

December 18   **As Much as Hearts Can Bear**

God's will is a great and infinite mystery—a thing of mighty mass and volume, which can no more be measured out to hungry souls in human sentences than the eternal knowledge of God or the boundless love of Christ. But even as there is a sense in which one poor human soul can hold enough of the eternal knowledge of God and the boundless love of Christ, so is there a sense in which God can put as much of His will into human words as human hearts can bear—as much as human will can will or human lives perform.   (6)

December 19   **The Final Test**

I say the final test of religion at the great Day is not religiousness, but Love; not what I have done, not what I have believed, not what I have achieved, but how I have discharged the common charities of life.   (21)

December 20   **In a Thirsty Land**

Men can be to other men as the shadow of a great rock in a thirsty land. Much more Christ; much more Christ as Perfect Man; much more still as Saviour of the World.   (23)

December 21   **Really Hungry?**

When a man goes to church really hungry and goes because he is hungry, he will pick up something, no matter where it is.   (11)

December 22   **Character and Conduct**

Character and conduct are never so vividly set before me as when in silence I bend in the presence of Christ, revealed not in wrath, but in love to me.   (1)

December 23   **Beginning of All Things**

The beginning of all things is in the will of God. The end of all things is in sanctification through faith in Jesus Christ. "By the which will ye are sanctified." Between these two poles all spiritual life and Christian experience run. And no motive outside Christ can lead a man to Christ. If your motive to holiness is not as high as Christ, it cannot make you rise to Christ. For water cannot rise above its level. (6)

December 24 Beauty Infinitely Real

Glory, then, is not something intangible or ghostly or transcendental. If it were this how could Paul ask men to reflect it? Stripped of its physical enswathement, it is beauty, moral and spiritual beauty—beauty infinitely real, infinitely exalted, yet infinitely near, and infinitely communicable. (1)

December 25 The Incarnation

The Incarnation was the eternal become temporal for a little while, that we might look at it. (27)

December 26 End of the Incarnation

With the Incarnation . . . we find how the Christ-Life has clothed Himself with matter, taken literal flesh, and dwelt among us. The Incarnation is the Life revealing the Type. Men are long since agreed that this is the end of the Incarnation—the revealing of God. But why should God be revealed? Why, indeed, but for man? Why but that "beholding as in a glass the glory of the only begotten we should be changed into the same Image"? (22)

December 27 The End of Life

What is the end of life? The end of life is not to do good, although many of us think so. It is not to win souls, although I once thought it so. The end of life is to do the will of God. (6)

December 28 As Clairvoyants

Heaven lies behind earth. This earth is not merely a place to live in, but to see in. We are to pass through it as clairvoyants, holding the whole temporal world as a vast transparency, through which the eternal shines. (6)

December 29   **Retrace Your Steps**

You must retrace your steps over that unburied past, and undo what you have done. You must go to the other lives which are stained with your blood-red stains and rub them out. Perhaps you did not lead them into their sin; but you did not lead them out of it. You did not show them you were a Christian. You left a worse memory with them than your real one. You pretended you were just like them—that your sources of happiness were just the same. You did not tell them you had a power which kept your life from Sin.   (6)

December 30   **What a Pace It Has Gone!**

This is the last letter of this year—what a pace it has all gone at! But—"he that doeth the will of God abideth for ever." This is the thing that lasts, so I will send it as the New Year text.   (14)

December 31   **A Day of Questions**

Tomorrow, the first day of a new year, is a day of *wishes*. Today, the last day of the old year, is a day of *questions*. Tomorrow is a time of anticipation; today is a time of reflection. Tomorrow our thoughts go out to the coming opportunities; today our minds wander among buried memories, and our hearts are full of self-questioning thoughts of what our past has been. If tomorrow is to be a time of resolution, today must be a day of investigation. *"What is your life?"*   (6)

REFERENCES

(1) *The Changed Life*

(2) *A Talk on Books*

(3) *What Is A Christian?*

(4) *The Study of the Bible*

(5) *Preparation for Learning*

(6) *The Ideal Life*

(7) *The Ideal Man*

(8) *Lessons from the Angelus*

(9) *A Life for a Life*

(10) *The New Evangelism*

(11) *Stones Rolled Away*

(12) *Spiritual Diagnosis*

(13) *Science to Christianity*

(14) *Various Letters*

(15) *Life on the Top Floor*

(16) *The Claims of Christianity*

(17) *A Talk with Open-Air Preachers*

(18) *The Life of Henry Drummond*—G. A. Smi.

(19) *Sermon—Funeral of Rev. John Ewing, Melbourne*

(20) *Expositor, 1885*

(21) *The Greatest Thing in the World*

(22) *Natural Law*

(23) *Pax Vobiscum*

(24) *First!*

(25) *How to Learn How*

(26) *Tropical Africa*

(27) *Miscellaneous Writings*

(28) *Dealing with Doubt*

(29) *The Ascent of Man*

(30) *The Man Who Is Down*

(31) *The City Without A Wall*

(32) *The Programme of Christianity*

(33) *The Three Facts of Salvation*

Henry Drummond had the unique distinction of being invited to give a series of addresses to a select audience of parliamentarians, academics, ecclesiastics and others of light and leading in the nation. He was asked to close the series with a prayer and did so in words of simplicity and beauty:

Lord Jesus, we have been talking to one another about Thee, and now we talk to Thee face to face. Thou art not far from any one of us. Thou art nearer than we are to one another, and Thou art saying to us, "Come unto Me, and I will give you rest." So we come just as we are. We pray Thee to remember us in Thy mercy and love. Take not Thy Spirit away from us, but enable us more and more to enter into the fellowship with Thyself. Bless all here who love the Lord Jesus in sincerity. Help those who love Thee not, and who miss Thee every day they live, here and now to begin their attachment and devotion to Thy person and service, for Thy name's sake, *Amen.*